IMAGES
of America

HISTORIC
DALLAS HOTELS

Dallas accommodations had come a long way by 1934, when this advertisement extolling the variety and quality of the city's hotels, motels, and tourist courts appeared in a publication directed to oil industry conventioneers. Having an adequate number of rooms and a range of prices were important economically, and city leaders knew it, often investing their own (and the taxpayers') money to see that Dallas's lodging was the very best.

ON THE COVER: The Statler Hilton was the first major hotel opened in Dallas after World War II. It boasted dozens of innovations not seen before in the city, including a heliport, piped-in elevator music, column-free ballrooms, and a dance floor that could be hydraulically raised or lowered. The main entrance, on Commerce Street, was Y-shaped, canopied, and lushly landscaped to provide a "luxurious, off-street driveway." (Texas/Dallas History and Archives Division Dallas Public Library)

IMAGES
of America

HISTORIC
DALLAS HOTELS

Sam Childers

ARCADIA
PUBLISHING

Published by Arcadia Publishing
Charleston SC, Chicago IL, Portsmouth NH, San Francisco CA

Printed in the United States of America

Library of Congress Control Number: 2009935856

For all general information contact Arcadia Publishing at:
Telephone 843-853-2070
Fax 843-853-0044
E-mail sales@arcadiapublishing.com
For customer service and orders:
Toll-Free 1-888-313-2665

Visit us on the Internet at www.arcadiapublishing.com

*To my parents, Sam and Connie, who always
encouraged my interest in our past.*

CONTENTS

ACKNOWLEDGMENTS

This book began as a paper that I presented at the annual *Legacies* Dallas History Conference in 2007 and in a subsequent profile of the Fairmont Hotel's legendary Venetian Room in another article for *Legacies: A History Journal for Dallas and North Central Texas*.

A great number of people assisted me in the completion of this book and I am grateful to each of them.

Kristie Kelly and Scott Davis at Arcadia Publishing guided me patiently throughout the process, and I am in their debt.

Sources for photographs were numerous, but I am particularly grateful to Jerome Sims at *The Dallas Morning News* and David Davis at the Adolphus Hotel, who were generous with their collections and time. Carol Roark and her staff at the Texas/Dallas History and Archives Division of the Dallas Public Library are an incredible resource. Dallas is fortunate to have their expertise and knowledge, and I encourage the reader to support our public library.

I am lucky to count as friends the finest historians in Dallas. Dr. Michael V. Hazel, who has provided me with many opportunities through the years, read the manuscript and provided much-appreciated advice. I can always count on the wise counsel of Dr. Thomas Smith and Dr. Darwin Payne as well.

My friend Ellen Zoudlik and Steve Noyes were lifesavers with scanning and technical issues, despite looming deadlines of their own. Evelyn Montgomery, Michael Aday, and Max Painter at Dallas Heritage Village located and scanned images from their collections, often at a moment's notice. Robert Allegrini with Hilton Hotels and Mark Young at the Hilton College at the University of Houston, hotel historians themselves, were tremendously helpful with suggestions and advice. Local photographer Jason Grant was generous in sharing his Statler photographs.

I am also deeply grateful to Shannah Milstead and Bill Armstrong, the Fairmont Dallas; Larry McAfee and Martha Conine, Warwick Melrose; Kate Neu, Stoneleigh Resort and Spa; Katie Bergfeld and Kristin Walker, Starwood Hotels and Resorts; Stephanie Hutson and Rebecca Morrison, Rosewood Hotels; Dana Berry, Magnolia; Jessica Jernigan, Old Red Museum; and Andrew Pena, Westin Hotels.

Finally, this book would not exist were it not for my family: Jeff, Delano, and Arthur—my love and gratitude go to them.

INTRODUCTION

From its earliest days, Dallas has provided lodging for the traveler. Although many consider Thomas Crutchfield's log cabin Dallas's first hotel, it was actually preceded by James Bryan's cabin and William Beeman's Dallas Tavern. As the years passed, newer and grander hotels enhanced Dallas's reputation as a modern, civilized, and cultured place to live and conduct business, and visitors to the city upon returning home spread the word that Dallas was much more cosmopolitan than was widely perceived.

City leaders have long recognized the importance of providing excellent accommodations and the role they play in presenting the image of a forward-looking city. The Adolphus Hotel was completed in 1912 by beer magnate Adolphus Busch despite his demands that leaders invest in the project and that the hotel be built on the site of city hall, an impressive and relatively new structure. The cash was raised and voters approved funding a new seat of local government. In the mid-20th century, construction of the Statler Hilton was financed by local businessmen who foresaw the need for modern hotels for Dallas's burgeoning convention business. Most recently, Dallas mayor Tom Leppert made the construction of a city-owned convention center hotel one of his highest priorities.

This book is a history of Dallas told through images and words about the hotels, motels, and tourist courts that have been, and in some cases still are, a part of the city's urban landscape and history. It is not a comprehensive study but is rather a narrative of dates and locations and of the men and women who built, financed, managed, and promoted these places. Some stories are well documented, and many notable events have occurred in Dallas's public accommodations, but the vast majority of remarkable moments reside in the mind of the reader, particularly those who have long called Dallas home. Dallas hotels have hosted presidents, entertainers, military leaders, political candidates, business moguls, and religious figures. They have also been the setting for proms, conventions, weddings, civic gatherings, Thanksgiving dinners, first dates, USO facilities, debutante balls, reunions, radio broadcasts, dances, and sadly, fires, explosions, suicides, and even funeral services.

This book is arranged chronologically, with one exception. The chapter "Roadside Attractions" is more subject-oriented; however, I have placed it between chapters covering the early 20th century ("Meet Me in the Lobby") and the 50-year period following World War II ("Wake-Up Call") as this era was the heyday of these businesses.

The first chapter, "Checking In," covers the time of Dallas's founding in 1841 to 1912, when the Adolphus Hotel opened, and recalls the "pioneer" Dallas hotels. The term "hotel" is used loosely here, for these accommodations were often crude, consisting of nothing more than a place to sleep on a log floor.

Initially, the book's format did not include a chapter focusing on any single hotel, but I have added "Five Star" focusing on the Adolphus. No hotel's story better affirms this book's theme, which is that Dallas business and political leaders saw to it that good hotels were built. It was an era when Dallas began to be seen as a cosmopolitan city, and the Adolphus stood out as a symbol of this prominence. In conducting research for this book, I discovered dozens of compelling images, many of which have never been previously published, that I felt should be seen. The Adolphus Hotel generously contributed many of these images from its archives.

In the third chapter, "Meet Me in the Lobby," Dallas was enjoying the fruits of technological advances along with the rest of the country, and innovations in architecture, transportation, building construction, and engineering made what seemed impossible just a few years earlier a reality. Hilton, one of the best-known names in the hotel industry, was practically born in Dallas in this period. There are a large number of images of the Statler Hilton, built in 1955–1956. The opening of the Statler, much like the Adolphus's debut, was a highly anticipated event. Its architecture was innovative, and it was another project that likely would have been unsuccessful without the intervention of business and political leaders. Both hotels represented cosmopolitan confidence. Interest in the preservation of the Statler is intense as the once futuristic edifice was named to the National Trust for Historic Preservation's "11 Most Endangered Historic Places" list in 2008.

The "Roadside Attractions" chapter discusses how Henry Ford's assembly line produced inexpensive automobiles that the "average man" could afford. Coupled with the seemingly overnight construction and improvement of roads and technological and labor advances that allowed the worker to enjoy more leisure time, the automobile led to an explosion of these roadside lodgings. As Dallas prepared to host the Texas Centennial Exposition in 1936, entrepreneurs saw the economic potential, and dozens of motels and motor courts were opened.

"Wake-Up Call" illustrates the newfound and forward-looking energy that followed years of economic hardship and a war that affected every Dallasite. Post-modern architecture and space age optimism left most Americans feeling that anything was possible, but two wars, disenfranchisement of many citizens, and dramatic feelings of unrest particularly in urban centers caused many to feel shaken. The population explosion of Dallas's suburban communities led to a decline of Dallas's urban core, and many of its grand hotels were left to decay out of neglect or demolished in the name of progress.

The final chapter, "Rise and Shine," illustrates how the city has seen a "hotel renaissance" of sorts in recent years. Several upscale hotels have been constructed, and local preservationists succeeded in enlightening investors and the public to the merits of rehabilitation of older buildings, including several hotels and historic properties that have been adapted to hotel use. They have not won every battle, and a great deal remains to be accomplished, but appreciation of these buildings is beginning to be seen as wise—not only as stewardship over our past but to the benefit of the bottom line as well.

Dallas continues to be a "hotel city." By 2009, the Uptown area had evolved into a second skyline composed of ultra-modern, "green" buildings, some of which are new hotels. A hotel dominated the local news in early 2009 when the debate over constructing a city-owned hotel at the Convention Center was front-page news. Despite a contentious and divided battle and a well-financed opposition campaign, voters approved the plan in May 2009.

One

CHECKING IN

They will continue to come just as long as we continue to keep our hotels in the lead.

—S. E. McIlhenny, former manager, Crutchfield House, 1910

The hotel accommodations of the city have always been excellent and it is believed that they are unexcelled today by any city in the South or West.

—*The Dallas Morning News*, October 1, 1905

Soon after John Neely Bryan settled on a bluff overlooking the Trinity River in 1841 and began planning the town of Dallas, other pioneers followed, and temporary housing was needed while they staked out their land and built their homes.

James Bryan, brother of the town's founder, arrived in the village of Dallas in 1846 and took in "guests" in his log cabin. William Beeman claimed that he opened the village's first inn, the Dallas Tavern, a small puncheon-floored house on the town square the next year. In 1852, four years before Dallas was chartered as a town, Thomas Crutchfield, one of Beeman's tenants, built a larger house on the northwest corner of the courthouse square, naming it Crutchfield House. It became renowned across the region for its accommodations, food, and livery stable and served as the town's early post office.

Sarah Horton Cockrell, widowed after her husband, Alexander, was killed, completed his Cockrell House (later St. Nicholas) hotel, which set the new standard for Dallas accommodations. Following a devastating 1860 fire, the town rebuilt and subsequent hotels opened, each enterprise striving to outdo the other.

Hotels were the center of the town's social life, hosting meetings, dances, and holiday celebrations. They housed saloons, restaurants, theaters, and ticket offices. They represented Dallas, and names of hotel arrivals were regularly printed in the newspapers.

The railroads arrived in the early 1870s, and most hotels were concentrated around the courthouse and train depots, but newer ones were built north and east as the town grew and neighborhoods changed. Demand for rooms escalated when Dallas secured the State Fair of Texas in 1886.

The apex of fine accommodations during this early period was reached when the Oriental Hotel opened in 1893. The site of Dallas's first two presidential visits, the Oriental was the city's premier hotel until the Adolphus Hotel opened in 1912.

A. Freeman, Artist.   Herald Print. Dallas.

CRUTCHFIELD HOUSE,

Thomas Crutchfield built the city's first substantial hotel and an adjoining livery stable, originally log structures, on the northwest corner of Main and Houston Streets in 1852. The hotel, along with much of the town, was destroyed in the fire of 1860. It was replaced with a two-story, antebellum structure a few hundred feet to the north at Main and Broadway. Constructed of brick and lumber hauled in from Buffalo Bayou, the hotel was the best known in the "Three Forks" region, as Dallas was commonly known then. Crutchfield House hosted Sam Houston, John Reagan, and Prince Paul of Germany—who stayed for two weeks in 1852. The hotel's parlor was the site of the formulation of a petition to the legislature for levying a tax to clear obstructions in the Trinity River. (Both, Dallas Historical Society.)

Sometime in the 1850s, warnings of an alleged Native American raid sounded throughout the town, and a group of armed men, including several residents of the Crutchfield House, raced to the banks of Turtle Creek, where the town was successfully defended. Crutchfield, an excellent marksman, provided food for his hotel's tables by hunting deer, buffalo, and quail in the countryside surrounding the town, and Crutchfield House became renowned for its fine food, which was prepared by his wife, Mariah, and a French cook whom they employed. Guests dined on "square meals" costing 25¢ and were summoned by a large bell until a drunken gunman shot it down. Crutchfield House, shown here in 1880, was destroyed by fire in 1888. (Dallas Public Library.)

Sarah H Cockrell

SARAH HORTON COCKRELL
1819 - 1892
TAKEN ABOUT 1890

Sarah Horton Cockrell was born in Virginia and moved to Texas in 1844. In 1847, she married Alexander Cockrell, and after his death in 1858, she managed and expanded his multiple enterprises including the Cockrell House, which he was in the process of building when he died. Upon its completion, it was renamed the St. Nicholas for the hotel's manager and former speaker of the Texas House, Nicholas Darnell. The St. Nicholas opened with a grand ball but was destroyed a year later in the fire of 1860. It was rebuilt at Commerce and Jefferson (now Record) Streets and renamed the Dallas and later the St. Charles Hotel. The St. Charles was razed in 1966 to construct the John F. Kennedy Memorial Plaza. (Left, Dallas Heritage Village; below, Dallas Historical Society.)

COCKRELL HOTEL AT DALLAS, TEXAS.

Commenced in the year 1857 by Alexander Cockrell. Continued and finished in year 1859 by Sarah Cockrell his wife.

Presented to Dallas Historical Society
by Monroe F. Cockrell, Sept. 1943

The St. James Hotel, built about 1872, occupied two floors above Taber Brothers Jewelers at Main and Murphy Streets. A fire in 1888 heavily damaged the jewelers, but the hotel did not burn. Guests were roused out of bed and leaped out of windows and used awnings to escape. All of the occupants survived, and credit was given to the prompt response of the fire department. (*The Dallas Morning News.*)

Tragedy was averted again in 1902 when the central portion of the structure collapsed at 2:00 a.m. on June 23, but all of its occupants managed to survive. It was rebuilt and remained on the site until 1923, when it was demolished to widen nearby Lamar Street shortly before this photograph was taken. The arrow in the photograph seems to indicate a paint store on the right. (Dallas Public Library.)

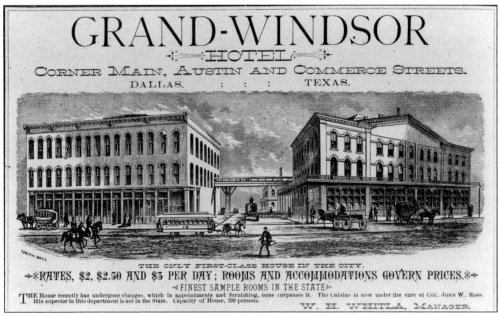

GRAND-WINDSOR

⁕ HOTEL ⁕

CORNER MAIN, AUSTIN AND COMMERCE STREETS.

DALLAS. : : : TEXAS.

THE ONLY FIRST-CLASS HOUSE IN THE CITY.

→⁕RATES, $2, $2.50 AND $3 PER DAY; ROOMS AND ACCOMMODATIONS GOVERN PRICES.⁕←

◄ FINEST SAMPLE ROOMS IN THE STATE ►

THE House recently has undergone changes, which in appointments and furnishing, none surpasses it. The Cuisine is now under the care of Col. John W. Ross. His superior in this department is not in the State. Capacity of House, 500 persons.

W. H. WHITLA, Manager.

The Le Grande hotel was built in 1875. Promoted as the "the most elegant hotel in the South," the Le Grande featured a huge gas chandelier in the lobby and an "electric annunciator" in each room to summon hotel staff. In 1879, the Le Grande's manager, Tom Smith, merged it with the Windsor (formerly the San Jacinto) and operated as the Grand Windsor. (Dallas Historical Society.)

Following the merger of the Le Grande and the Windsor, a wooden bridge was constructed across Austin Street that was eventually enclosed and carpeted and became a prime viewing location of parades and other public events. The hotel featured one of the first elevators in the city. A hall on the second floor served for some time as the town's theater. (*The Dallas Morning News.*)

The Grand Windsor's fortress-style construction included 18-inch-thick masonry walls. Although it was known as one of the finest hotels in the region, hotel guests in late-19th-century Dallas took baths at public bathhouses, since hot water had to be obtained by the pitcher in the lobby, and laundry was sent out to local Chinese laundrymen. (*The Dallas Morning News.*)

The Grand Windsor was the site of many of the state's early political conventions and meetings. In 1894, Charles Culberson was nominated as the Democrats' candidate for governor here. (*The Dallas Morning News.*)

St. George Hotel Annex, Dallas, Texas.

The Grand Windsor occupied most of the block where the Katy Building stands at Commerce and Market Streets. The hotel was slowly demolished over the years until only one section (extreme right) of the 18-inch-thick masonry walls remained. This remnant operated as, among other things, a liquor store, a café, a travel bureau, and a garage. The last section was razed in 1950 for a parking lot. (*The Dallas Morning News.*)

The St. George opened in 1875 as the Lamar Hotel at Commerce and Martin Streets. It originally was a four-story structure with a mansard roof and was later extensively expanded. Manager Tom Smith (formerly of the Grand Windsor, see page 14) referred to it as the "unabridged" in reference to the Grand Windsor's most notable feature. (Author's collection.)

H. P. Mozier designed an eight-story annex in 1909 that doubled the size of the hotel. The addition included a new arcade entry from Main Street. Later foresighted hotel operators such as Ben Whittaker anticipated the lucrative potential the Texas Centennial City would bring. Whittaker purchased the hotel in 1935 following owner William Diamond's death and renamed it the Whitmore. He invested $100,000 to remodel and install apartments on the roof. (Dallas Heritage Village.)

New Annex of The St. George Hotel, Charles Hodges, Prop., Dallas, Texas.

In 1934, hotel manager Walter Williams was murdered by an intoxicated employee, Aaron Shults, in the hotel's kitchen. Shults awoke later in jail and claimed to remember nothing about the crime. According to police, he said, "I sure hate it. He was a fine old man." The building (extreme left) was razed in 1974 for development of Three Main Place, which was never built. (Dallas Heritage Village.)

The Cliff Hotel at Jefferson and Crawford Streets was built by Thomas Marsalis in 1889. Modeled after Adirondack resorts, it furnished "a cool resort for Texas people in the summer and warm resort for Northern people in winter." It became the all-female Oak Cliff College in 1892 and reconverted to the Cliff Hotel in 1907. Later renamed the Forest Inn, it was demolished in 1945. (*The Dallas Morning News.*)

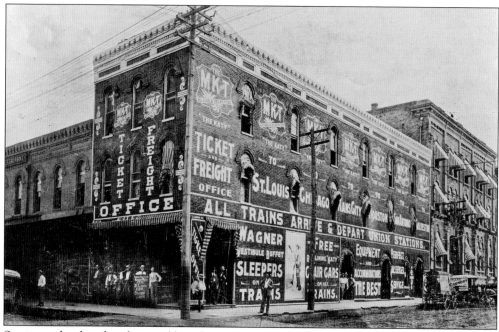

Services such as laundries, livery stables, tobacconists, taverns, and restaurants were often located near the town's hotels. This photograph of the MKT ticket office at Lamar and Main Streets was taken about 1890 and shows a portion of the Lamar House on the left side of the image. Lamar House catered to long- and short-term residents and was known for its excellent Sunday dinners. (*The Dallas Morning News.*)

Capt. J. B. McLeod opened the 143-room McLeod Hotel on Main Street in April 1890 but died before the end of the year, when his wife took over its management. One of Dallas's first tall buildings, the seven-story hotel was considered a skyscraper. The first floor held an elegant, popular billiard room. The posters on the adjacent building advertise the 1892 State Fair of Texas. (*The Dallas Morning News.*)

J. B. McLeod's widow sold the hotel not long after her husband's death, and after changing hands several times, it was refurbished and renamed the Imperial Hotel in 1904. It was referred to as a "drummers' hotel," popular with traveling salesmen, who were called "drummers" for "beating the drum" for whatever product they were selling. The First Unitarian Church was organized at the McLeod. (Dallas Public Library.)

Imperial Hotel, Dallas.

A fire severely damaged the hotel in 1914, and it was purchased by the American Exchange National Bank. Uninhabitable, the ruins were propped up and remained there until 1916, when the bank acquired adjacent properties and then tore down the hotel to make way for the new bank headquarters. (Dallas Heritage Village.)

Early hotels in Dallas often doubled as saloons or taverns. The City Hotel, built in 1892 and located at 2528 Elm Street, was one such establishment. In 1911, owner S. W. Everett was cited for keeping his bar open on Sunday. The building, shown in a contemporary photograph, is probably the oldest hotel building existing in Dallas today. The cast-iron front has seven bays with two storefronts. (Photograph by the author.)

Thomas Field came to Texas from Missouri in 1872 and was instrumental in securing the Texas and Pacific Railroad for Dallas. He is credited with originating and supporting the location of the state fairgrounds on its present site. Once called "the Father of Oak Cliff," he was one of the first developers there. In 1889, he chartered the Oriental Hotel Company and announced plans to build a six-story luxury hotel. The Oriental Hotel was nearly completed by 1893 when Field, a victim of the financial panic that year, sold his interest to a group of investors headed by St. Louis beer magnate Adolphus Busch. Busch completed the hotel and opened the doors in October just in time for the state fair. Field became less active after the financial panic and died in 1909. Field Street in downtown Dallas was named for him in 1938. (Dallas Historical Society.)

In March 1887, Field purchased the Robert Williams home with its terraced lawn at Commerce and Akard Streets with plans to develop a hotel in an area that was removed from similar establishments. He moved the home, leveled the site, and began construction despite the plans being labeled "Field's Folly," as many thought the site was too far into the country. (*The Dallas Morning News.*)

The Oriental opened with a huge public celebration attended by nearly every notable person in the city. The hotel featured every available luxury and appointment: the ground-floor lobby was complete with marble floors and wainscoting, massive pillars, a grand staircase, and a "profusion of beautiful plants" and "would seem to make it appear that the hotel was oriental in nature as well as in name," according to *The Dallas Morning News.* (*The Dallas Morning News.*)

ORIENTAL HOTEL.

5953. COPYRIGHT, 1903, BY JOSEPH LINZ AND BROS., DALLAS, TEX.

The Oriental's ground floor contained a grand dining room, a barbershop, a cigar stand, billiard rooms, and a huge barroom with one of the first tile floors in the city. The second floor held parlors and a bridal room. The building featured elevators and was completely electric. For years, it was considered the finest hotel in Dallas. It was torn down in 1924 to make way for the Baker Hotel. (*The Dallas Morning News.*)

Dallas experienced its first presidential visit when Theodore Roosevelt stopped briefly in 1905. He paraded through downtown to the Oriental, where dozens of children filled the windows. After platform remarks, he retired to a suite before attending a banquet in his honor. The presidential table featured a floral battleship floating in Trinity River water. (Dallas Historical Society.)

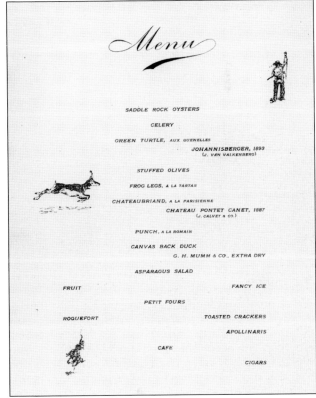

Menu

SADDLE ROCK OYSTERS

CELERY

GREEN TURTLE, AUX QUENELLES

JOHANNISBERGER, 1893
(J. VAN VALKENBERG)

STUFFED OLIVES

FROG LEGS, A LA TARTAR

CHATEAUBRIAND, A LA PARISIENNE

CHATEAU PONTET CANET, 1887
(J. CALVET & CO.)

PUNCH, A LA ROMAIN

CANVAS BACK DUCK

G. H. MUMM & CO., EXTRA DRY

ASPARAGUS SALAD

FRUIT

FANCY ICE

PETIT FOURS

ROQUEFORT

TOASTED CRACKERS

APOLLINARIS

CAFE

CIGARS

An elaborate dinner at the Oriental for Pres. William Howard Taft's 1909 visit featured a multi-course banquet. The corpulent Taft expressed to Mayor Stephen Hay his "pleasant surprise" at the steak and went at it "with vim and appetite that indicated how thoroughly he enjoyed the whole thing." Taft had requested that dinner be served quickly, and the hotel's double-shift staff of waiters served all the guests in 38 minutes. (Dallas Historical Society.)

Before modern electronic communications were a part of everyday life, the written letter and the telegraph were the primary means of connecting with friends and business associates. This ornately designed letterhead from the Oriental Hotel provided stationery to guests but also was a form of free advertising for the hotel. (Author's collection.)

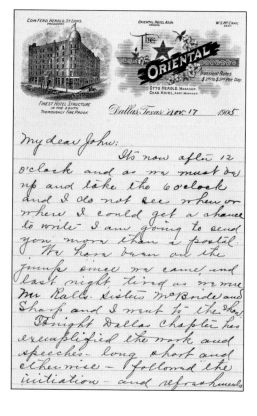

The Oriental Hotel's position as the finest hotel in Dallas is indicated by the expansive newsstand located on the sidewalk on Commerce Street. The hotel was the most expensive and exclusive in the city, and its clientele were typically educated, upper-class professionals and businessmen. (Dallas Public Library.)

The Majestic was the first of several "apartment hotels" built in Dallas after the turn of the 20th century. Thomas Naracrosse constructed the five-story hotel near City Park in 1905. Designed by Earle Silven, it was considered the city's first "suburban" hotel. This photograph shows the hotel nearing completion. (*The Dallas Morning News.*)

The Majestic was designed in Italian Renaissance style and contained 50 apartments. The top floor held a café and dining room, and a rooftop promenade "which may be used for amusement attractions" capped the building. Its status as Dallas's most modern hotel was confirmed in 1905 when it hosted the Bachelor's German Club reception and the prestigious Idlewild Club Ball. (Dallas Heritage Village.)

Ambassador Apartment Hotel

In 1907, the Majestic was purchased by J. S. Kendall, who renamed it the Park Hotel, and in 1933, it was completely renovated and called the Ambassador Hotel. Architect Anton Kron supervised a renovation of the building that clad the hotel in stucco and added a tile roof. It was later converted to a home for senior citizens and today houses the Dallas Ministry Center. (Dallas Heritage Village.)

The Allen Hotel was built sometime around 1908 and, along with the former City Hotel building, is one of the oldest cast-iron-front buildings remaining in Dallas. Its name was changed to the Boyd Hotel and was a popular hotel for musicians performing in Deep Ellum. Today the Local Restaurant is in this location. (Photograph by the author.)

John Parkinson designed the Southland Hotel at Main and Murphy Streets in 1907. It was the first "skyscraper" in the city to use steel-framed construction and was considered so fireproof that owner J. W. Hunt said "money spent on fire insurance would be thrown away." It had a drinking fountain that dispensed cold water through a figure of Venus and was the nation's second hotel with running ice water in every room. (Dallas Heritage Village.)

HOTEL SOUTHLAND, DALLAS, TEX.

Many of the Southland's features were new innovations reflecting technological advances that made many of the era's day-to-day tasks easier and more convenient. The hotel was the first in the country to offer mail chutes on each floor that deposited guests' mail directly into a basement postal office and included "the apparatus for cleaning the rooms and carpets by the vacuum air process." (Dallas Heritage Village.)

The hotel's mahogany-paneled bar was decorated with three murals, and the ground floor held a restaurant, a writing room, a drugstore, a haberdasher, and a "ladies parlor" (below). The basement contained a billiard room, barbershop, and another innovation—a beauty parlor where "a lady may arrange her dress or hat properly." (Old Red Museum of Dallas County History and Culture.)

The Southland ranked second only to the Oriental and shortly after its opening battled the Oriental for the honor of hosting Vice Pres. Charles Fairbanks, who visited the state fair in October. The Oriental won, but the Southland hosted Gov. Thomas Campbell, who arrived in Dallas to welcome the vice president. The hotel underwent a major renovation prior to the Centennial festivities in 1936. During World War II servicemen were banned from the hotel by order of the city council's venereal disease control committee, making it the largest hotel in the city placed off limits. The hotel stood until 1971 when it was torn down to make way for construction of One Main Place. (Dallas Heritage Village.)

HOTEL WALDORF, 1302 COMMERCE STREET, DALLAS, TEXAS.

The Waldorf Hotel was constructed in 1911 at Commerce and Kendall (now closed) Streets and expanded in 1919. Conrad Hilton purchased the Waldorf in 1922, his fourth hotel purchase in Texas and his first in Dallas. Hilton added a 12-story annex and renamed it the Bluebonnet Hotel. It was acquired by the City State Bank in 1959 and torn down that year to construct a bank and office building. (Dallas Heritage Village.)

A. W. Campbell came to Dallas in 1872 and became wealthy buying and selling downtown real estate. He built one of the first brick homes in Dallas at Elm and Harwood Streets and replaced it in 1911 with a five-story hotel designed by Otto Lang. In the 1920s, it was owned by Texan Jesse Jones, who served as Secretary of Commerce and chairman of the Reconstruction Finance Corporation under Pres. Franklin Roosevelt. (Dallas Public Library.)

Two

FIVE STAR

We will build a twenty-story building which will be a credit to your city and which should turn a good interest to those who have made the investment.

—Adolphus Busch, June 11, 1910

That twenty-story hotel will be a great milestone—a new monument to the Dallas spirit.

—*The Dallas Morning News*, October 10, 1910

It was to be called the New Oriental. When Dallas citizens learned that Adolphus Busch, one of the wealthiest men in the country, welcomed the proposal put forth by their elected officials to construct a grand tower "addition" to his Oriental Hotel, they jumped at the opportunity. Talk in the summer of 1910 focused on little else. The old Oriental had represented Dallas well, but despite its relatively young age of 19, it seemed dowdy and dated.

Dallas was an exciting and optimistic city in that year. In September, official census tabulations numbered its inhabitants at 92,104, an increase of 116 percent from the previous decade. Boosters were exhilarated that Dallas had more new roads, telephones, and businesses than any other city in the state. Dallas officials attempted to harness and manage the evolution. In 1909, the chamber of commerce established the City Plan and Improvement League and hired George Kessler to devise a long-range civic improvement plan, "The City Plan for Dallas." His recommendations included stemming flooding of the Trinity River, establishing parks and plazas, and removing dangerous railroad crossings and narrow downtown streets. In short, Kessler sought to tame Dallas.

Busch's proposal for a baroque palace melded perfectly with the confident and hopeful attitude of Dallas's people. The New Oriental would be built regardless of what had to be done. It happened quickly and with little opposition. On May 22, 1910, Mayor Stephen Hay and four prominent Dallas businessmen met with the beer magnate in St. Louis to propose the hotel idea. Two days later, *The Dallas Morning News* headline read, "20-Story Hotel For This City—City Hall To Be Sold."

Mayor Stephen Hay, accompanied by prominent citizens Henry Lindsey, Charles Bolanz, and F. V. Tryon, traveled to St. Louis in May 1910 to lobby Adolphus Busch to build a huge addition to the Oriental Hotel. Busch agreed, but he desired the site opposite the Oriental—even though it was occupied by city hall. The committee agreed to the deal on the spot. There was little opposition; city offices relocated to temporary quarters at 411 Commerce Street, and demolition began in October. A month later, the task was completed. In January 1911, the site for the new city hall was selected, a block occupied by the Central Presbyterian Church on Harwood Street between Main and Commerce Streets. (Dallas Public Library.)

The hotel was originally to be called the New Oriental Hotel. The chamber of commerce telegraphed Busch in March 1911 suggesting that it be named the Adolphus in his honor. Busch responded, "I shall cheerfully acquiesce and be proud of it." (The Adolphus Archives.)

In October 1911 when this photograph was taken, the steel framework was completed and exterior brickwork had begun on the lower floors. Architect Tom Barnett of Barnett, Haynes, and Barnett of St. Louis spent most of the year in Dallas supervising the construction. In December, a labor strike briefly halted work but it resumed before the New Year began. On December 28, 1911, the cornerstone was officially laid. (*The Dallas Morning News*.)

The Adolphus changed the face of the Dallas skyline and became its tallest building, surpassing the Praetorian by 40 feet. Architect Barnett spared no expense on the $1.8-million palace. Designed in the Louis XIV style, the structure's base was of red granite and the exterior was clad in Oriental tapestry brick and gray granite. The mansard roof was comprised of variegated slate crested with antiqued bronze. At the 15th floor, two massive allegorical figures representing "Morning" and "Night" were sculpted by noted Chicago artist Leon Hermant. The primary entrance from Commerce Street was topped with a balcony, and an arcade opened through the first two stories, providing glimpses of the interior from the street. The secondary entrance on Akard Street was crowned with reliefs of Mercury and Ceres. The entire building was designed with the Texas climate in mind with ample windows on every floor to admit fresh air. (*The Dallas Morning News.*)

This early piece of Adolphus marketing read like a recruitment advertisement for new residents. (Note the auto passenger saying, "I would love to live here.") Hardly an aspect of life in Dallas was omitted as the piece touts the quality of schools, churches, country clubs, roads, buildings, train schedules, parks, homes, and amusements. (The Adolphus Archives.)

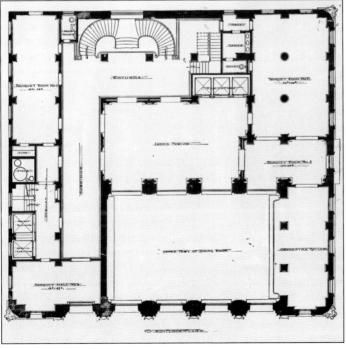

The first three floors of the hotel were public rooms containing dining rooms, ballrooms, and parlors. Both street entrances led to a three-story rotunda and a lobby containing a cigar stand, newsstand, drugstore, and clothing boutiques. In this plan of the third floor, stairs from the rotunda can be seen at the top center. Other rooms were reserved for a ladies' parlor, four banquet rooms, and an orchestra gallery. (The Adolphus Archives.)

This view of the main dining room shows the Louis XIV design carried into the interior of the hotel. Arched vaults admit light, as do the French doors on the right. The entire room was decorated in relief; particularly beautiful are the figures of women, arms outstretched, above the second-level gallery. (*The Dallas Morning News.*)

The hotel's lobby was designed to impress visitors and to reflect the Adolphus's status as the finest hotel in the city. It was paneled in walnut, and bronze light fixtures were colored antique gold. In addition to full-sized shops, guests were able to purchase candy, cigars, postcards, and other small items at glass-fronted counters located near the elevators. (*The Dallas Morning News.*)

Adolphus Hotel
Commerce and Akard Sts.
Dallas, Texas

Sadly, Adolphus Busch died in 1913. His family continued to operate the hotel, and in 1916, Lang and Witchell designed a 12-story addition to the west of the original building that architecturally complemented Barnett's original design, although far less ornamented. The addition was completed in 1917 and added 229 rooms, bringing the total to more than 500. The addition became known as the "Junior Adolphus." In addition to expanded capacity and hotel amenities, the annex's rooftop provided space for a restaurant and entertainment venue called Bambooland. This photograph was taken in 1924 just prior to the hotel's third expansion, which would add a 22-story addition, "Adolphus III," immediately behind the original tower. In the extreme foreground, the site of the Oriental Hotel can be seen just after it was demolished for construction of the Baker Hotel. (*The Dallas Morning News.*)

Dominating the lobby space was a grand staircase of pink Tennessee marble and antiqued bronze. Numerous tapestries and works of art, some from Adolphus Busch's personal collection, hung from the walls, and light was admitted through a large stained-glass window on the stair landing. (*The Dallas Morning News.*)

In the 1920s, the Adolphus hosted nearly every notable person of the era who visited Dallas, including Rudolph Valentino, Babe Ruth, Amelia Earhart, Charles Lindbergh, Warren G. Harding, William Howard Taft, and Harry Houdini. Gen. John J. Pershing, a guest in 1920, kissed five-year-old Clarice Gardner in the lobby and, smiling at the child's mother, said, "It's a hard matter to keep from kissing some of the older ones." (*The Dallas Morning News.*)

This postcard shows the original 1912 Adolphus (right), the 1917 Junior Adolphus addition (left), and the 1924 Adolphus III tower. Alfred C. Bossom's design blended harmoniously with the other buildings, and the addition of 325 rooms made it the largest hotel in the state of Texas. An entrance from Main Street was added, making it possible to go from Main to Commerce Street without leaving the hotel. (Author's collection.)

An exotic Adolphus dining spot was the Spa and Chinese Restaurant, adjacent to the Junior Adolphus lobby. A 1924 newspaper review said, "To insure real Oriental viands, a staff of Chinese cooks is employed. The atmosphere of the Orient pervades the spa, and to dine there is said to be like spending an evening in old Pekin [*sic*]." (The Adolphus Archives.)

The Adolphus added six kitchens after it was expanded in 1924. In addition to the main kitchen, there were five banquet kitchens, a lunchroom kitchen, an ice cream shop, and a bakery that produced 5,000 rolls, 1,000 loaves of bread, and 250 pies daily. The hotel's catering and banquet facilities were constantly busy as the Adolphus became a popular setting for club meetings and conventions. (The Adolphus Archives.)

The Adolphus lunchroom was added when the hotel was expanded and was heavily patronized by downtown workers and shoppers. (The Adolphus Archives.)

Although spartan (and crazily multi-patterned) by today's standards, this typical guest room was luxurious in the 1920s. Steam heat was provided by the radiator against the wall, and a ceiling fan, combined with open windows, circulated the air and cooled the rooms in the summer. Even the smallest apartments were equipped with a writing desk, marble-topped dresser, nightstand, and a telephone. (The Adolphus Archives.)

This photograph shows Bambooland sometime in the 1920s. Rooftop gardens were popular gathering places in the era before air-conditioning, and soon after the Baker opened, it launched a rival venue, the Peacock Terrace. WFAA-Radio broadcast musical performances from Bambooland for many years. (The Adolphus Archives.)

Adolphus guests had every possible convenience within the hotel, including a tile-floored, six-chair barbershop, located in the hotel's basement. In addition to haircuts, male guests could get a shave, a shoe shine, or a manicure. (The Adolphus Archives.)

Like the barbershop, the presence of spittoons indicated that the bar was a bastion of male guests, but the room fell silent after Prohibition became the law in 1919. Even the Busch family was not above suspicion. In 1920, while staying at the hotel, Adolphus Busch III had two trunks seized by agents who suspected that they contained illegal whisky. No charges were filed, and he called the actions "un-American and high-handed." (The Adolphus Archives.)

Dallas has long been a center for trade markets and merchandise showrooms. Before the Dallas Market Center and Dallas Trade Marts were built in the 1950s and 1960s, trade shows were held at the Santa Fe Annex Building, the state fairgrounds, and local hotels. This photograph taken at the Adolphus in the early 1920s shows market samples of what appear to be grooming kits designed for travel. (The Adolphus Archives.)

Attracting local clientele was an important part of the competitive hotel business. In 1936, the Adolphus opened the Century Room that became, along with the Baker's Mural Room, popular with centennial visitors as well as locals. In its heyday from the 1930s through the 1950s, the Century Room offered three shows daily. One of the most popular and well-remembered acts was the Ice Revue starring Dorothy Franey Langkop. (The Adolphus Archives.)

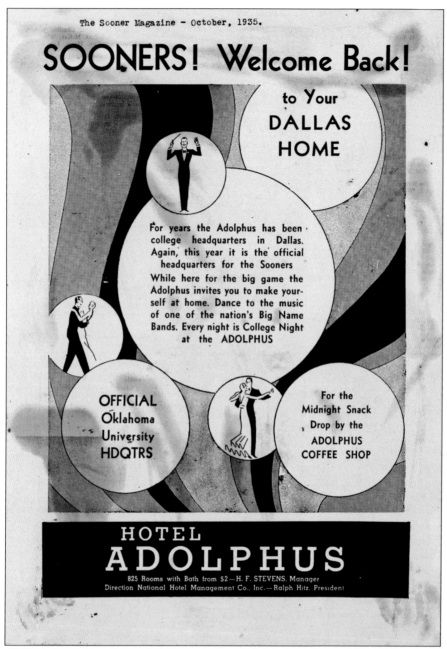

Since 1900, the annual gridiron clash between the Oklahoma Sooners and the Texas Longhorns has brought tens of thousands of rabid fans to downtown Dallas, where, until 1992, Commerce Street was the center of the revelry. One team typically stayed at the Adolphus and the other across Commerce at the Baker. Parties, pep rallies, and banquets completely took over both hotels, which were decorated in either crimson or burnt orange. Commerce Street was impassable as cars crawled slowly up and down the street, and sidewalks were a crush of rowdy, often drunken football fans. Often, when shouting and name calling got fans nowhere, they retreated to their hotel rooms, and mattresses and furniture rained down on the crowd. (The Adolphus Archives.)

In 1916, the U.S. military banned alcohol consumption by its troops, and three years later, national prohibition became the law. Anheuser-Busch began producing Bevo beer, a non-alcoholic "cereal beverage," as a means to stay afloat financially. The Busch family, who would control the Adolphus until 1949, naturally served Bevo. Bevo's mascot was Renard Fox, based on a medieval character of French literature. (The Adolphus Archives.)

Apparently, the live music played in Bambooland and the Century Room was so catchy that patrons had to be warned of the perils of dancing in the aisles with one of these small cards placed on each table. One of the most popular acts at the Adolphus was Phil Harris and His Movie Star Orchestra. Harris, along with Leah Ray, "The Most Beautiful Girl in Radio," gained a large local following. (The Adolphus Archives.)

week nights or $1.10 Saturdays
with a cover charge of 85 cents
After 9 p. m. all service is a la carte

⇑

dinner before 9 p. m.
No cover charge to guests who order

Please Leave Aisles Open

Guests are requested to refrain from dancing in the aisles. If you disregard this warning, we are not responsible for accidents, as colliding with waiters

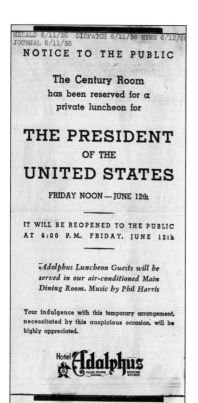

NOTICE TO THE PUBLIC

The Century Room

has been reserved for a
private luncheon for

THE PRESIDENT
OF THE
UNITED STATES

FRIDAY NOON — JUNE 12th

IT WILL BE REOPENED TO THE PUBLIC
AT 6:00 P.M., FRIDAY, JUNE 12th

*Adolphus Luncheon Guests will be
served in our air-conditioned Main
Dining Room. Music by Phil Harris*

Your indulgence with this temporary arrangement,
necessitated by this auspicious occasion, will be
highly appreciated.

Hotel **Adolphus**

Pres. Franklin Roosevelt visited Dallas in June 1936 to open the Texas Centennial Exposition with an address at the Cotton Bowl. Later he was honored at a luncheon in the Century Room. *The Dallas Morning News* called it "one of the most important events in the history of the city." (The Adolphus Archives.)

*In Honor of
The President of the United States*

Mrs. Henry B. Decherd

Nearly every prominent man in Dallas was invited to the presidential luncheon. At the Adolphus, FDR used back elevators to conceal his paralysis and leaned on his son Elliot as he entered the floral-bedecked ballroom. In brief remarks, Roosevelt said, "I always regret the fact that I seem to be always getting off a train or on a train and I have no time to stop or visit." (Dallas Historical Society.)

The Adolphus was purchased from Busch heirs in 1949 by Leo Corrigan, a Dallas real estate investor and developer. Corrigan announced plans in June 1950 to add a third tower addition to the Adolphus and to completely air condition the entire complex, making it the largest air-conditioned hotel in the world. Architect Wyatt Hedrick designed the least cohesive of the three additions, a 24-story, buff-colored structure completely unadorned except for a huge illuminated "Adolphus" sign at the top. The building was designed so as not to be seen from the hotel's Commerce Street side. This photograph shows Main Street looking east in the early 1950s. For a short time after the addition was completed, the Adolphus was the largest hotel in the country with nearly 1,300 rooms. (*The Dallas Morning News*.)

The Adolphus underwent a $60-million restoration in 1980 that returned much of the grandeur to the building. On the hotel's 75th birthday in 1987, Dallas mayor Annette Strauss assisted Grady Harris (right) and June Robinson (rear) in unveiling a marker designating the Adolphus as a city landmark. They were employees of the hotel for 30 and 27 years respectively. At left, Dallas Landmark Commission chairman Robert Canavan looked on. (*The Dallas Morning News.*)

As the Adolphus prepares to celebrate its centennial in 2012, it continues to represent the sophistication and hospitality of Dallas and remains one of the finest hotels in the city. Hotel staff report that first-time visitors continue to marvel at the architecture and decor. (Dallas Heritage Village.)

Three

MEET ME IN THE LOBBY

Nothing more accurately indicates the stages of growth of a city than its hotels.

—D. C. McCord, Dallas building inspector, February 27, 1926

Just how many of the 15,000 people that have represented Dallas's population gain annually for several years may be traced to our excellent hotels cannot be ascertained.

—*Dallas*, official publication of the Dallas Chamber of Commerce, February 1925

The half-century between the opening of the Adolphus and the debut of the Statler saw the hotels' function remain essentially the same, but rapid advances in technology provided guests with a great variety of safer, cleaner, and more comfortable accommodations.

Many hotels led local efforts for civic responsibility and even social change. During World War I, hotels sponsored "meatless" and "wheatless" days to conserve food for the war effort. Hotel workers had been trying for many years to organize during the Progressive Era and were finally successful in 1922. Despite these noble causes, hotel operators were in the business to make money and sometimes flaunted the law. During Prohibition, it was generally known that a downtown hotel was an easy place to obtain illicit whiskey, and hotel management defiantly resisted public officials' efforts to ban the sale of "set-ups" (essentially cracked ice and ginger ale).

The development of good roads and the affordability of the automobile saw establishments such as the Melrose and the Stoneleigh open as "apartment hotels" that blended the amenities of home with the convenience and prestige of a "big city" hotel.

The most significant year of this period was 1925, which saw yet another major expansion of the Adolphus, the openings of the Hotel Scott and of the fondly remembered Baker, and the origins of an enterprise that would become practically synonymous with the word "hotel."

DALLAS HAS

DALLAS HOTEL ASSOCIATION
MEMBERSHIP ROSTER

THE AMBASSADOR	CLIFF HOTEL	THE JEFFERSON HOTEL	SOUTHLAND HOTEL
BAKER HOTEL	DALLAS ATHLETIC CLUB	MAYFAIR HOTEL	THE STONELEIGH
BLUE BONNET HOTEL	THE ERVINGTON HOTEL AND APARTMENTS	MELROSE HOTEL	THE TEXAN HOTEL
CAMPBELL HOTEL	HILTON HOTEL	SANGER HOTEL AND APARTMENTS	WHITMORE HOTEL
CLIFFTON HOTEL AND APARTMENTS	HOTEL ADOLPHUS	SCOTT HOTEL	WORTH HOTEL

The hotel business was highly competitive, but owners and operators realized that an organization to promote their properties and lobby for common interests was needed. In 1903, the Texas Hotel Keepers Association was founded at the Oriental Hotel. In 1922, the Dallas Hotel Men's Association was organized to "co-operate with other business organizations in the upbuilding of Dallas and to take an active part in all civic activities." Otto Herrold of the Adolphus was elected its first president. By 1936, when this advertisement ran, the group had changed its name to the Dallas Hotel Association and claimed 20 member hotels. (The Adolphus Archives.)

50

Ohioan Charles Mangold moved to Dallas in 1885 where he established a wholesale and retail liquor business. An enthusiastic Oak Cliff booster, Mangold promoted arts and culture, developed Lake Cliff Park, led the establishment of the Oak Cliff Little Theater, and promoted the construction of the first permanent viaduct between Oak Cliff and Dallas, in addition to building the Jefferson Hotel. He is shown here with Jefferson bartenders in 1933. (Dallas Public Library.)

Constructed with Texas materials and opened in October 1917, the Hotel Jefferson was state of the art for its time. One floor was reserved for "the exclusive use of women unattended, no men being quartered on that floor." Mangold related that on opening day, a woman arriving in Dallas said she had been told the city was uncouth, but her first impression, "through the Jefferson, was an agreeable surprise." (Author's collection.)

HOTEL JEFFERSON
DALLAS, TEXAS

Dallas's Union Station was completed in 1916 and consolidated the five depots and nine railroads serving the city into a single Beaux Arts terminal. The Jefferson was strategically situated across from the depot so that the traveler crossed Ferris Plaza, George Kessler's "front door to Dallas," to reach the hotel. Named for Royal Ferris, who served on the committee that lobbied for the construction of the terminal, the park was completed in 1921. (Author's collection.)

Travelers arriving at Union Station needed only to cross Houston Street to find clean, comfortable accommodations. The location was ideal for transient visitors such as traveling salesmen and was particularly busy during the annual State Fair of Texas. Efforts were made to create a home-like atmosphere, and each room was equipped with glass-topped bureaus and dressing tables and "Brussels and Axminster rugs covering the floors." (Author's collection.)

The Jefferson proved so profitable that an extensive addition was begun in 1919. Completed in 1921, the expansion tripled the size of the hotel and boasted "the largest hotel lobby in Dallas." By the 1940s, a massive Dr. Pepper advertising sign with its prewar "Good For Life" slogan had been added to the roof. Dr. Pepper, although invented in Waco, was based in Dallas for many years. Dr. Pepper's annual stockholders' meeting was often held at the Jefferson, which perhaps explains the sign's prominent perch. The Dr. Pepper and Hotel Jefferson signs both faced west toward Union Station's arriving passengers and approaching trains, as well as cars crossing the viaduct from Oak Cliff. (*The Dallas Morning News.*)

In 1953, the Jefferson was leased to Alsonett Hotels, which owned, among other properties, the Peabody Hotel in Memphis. It underwent a massive renovation that added air-conditioning and a drive-in "motor entrance." The Dr. Pepper sign was removed, and "Hotel Dallas" signs sprouted from the roof. Another sign, in script lettering to blend in with *The Dallas Morning News* sign across Ferris Plaza, was added to the south facade. (*The Dallas Morning News.*)

The Stoneleigh Court opened in 1923 and was hailed as "the South's finest apartment hotel." Costing $1.5 million, the Beaux Arts hotel was designed by F. J. Woener, and upon its completion, it was one of the tallest hotels west of the Mississippi. The hotel consisted of 135 suites with kitchenettes and Murphy beds. A self-contained "city within a hotel," its amenities included beauty and barbershops, a grocery store, and a children's gymnasium. (The Stoneleigh Hotel and Spa.)

In 1934, the Stoneleigh was purchased by Col. Harry Stewart, Texas distributor for Ford Motor tractors and farm implements. He retained architects LaRoche and Dahl to design a 12th-floor, 7,500-square-foot penthouse addition as a home for himself and his family. The penthouse became legendary for its hidden rooms and secret passageways allegedly added as a means for a quick exit from Stewart's late-night poker games. (The Stoneleigh Hotel and Spa.)

The dust had barely settled on the Stoneleigh Court when construction began on nearby Maple Terrace apartments. Designed by Alfred Bossom and Thompson and Swaine, the eight-story structure was built on the sites of the Royal A. Ferris home and later of the 1892 George Dilley mansion, considered one of the finest old homes in Dallas. The Maple Terrace opened in 1925. (Author's collection.)

Harry Stewart hired noted interior designer Dorothy Draper to conceive an elegant apartment reminiscent of a formal English manor home, combined with subtle art deco elements. No expense was spared as Stewart and his wife, Edith, imported 500-year-old oak paneling from the Charterhouse School in London and installed Italian marble floors throughout the penthouse. (The Stoneleigh Hotel and Spa.)

In 1923, Dorothy Draper established the first interior design firm in the country, considered daring at the time, since few women worked professionally. Born into a prominent New York family, she counted Eleanor Roosevelt among her childhood friends. Her specialty was public spaces, and she created interiors for several large hotels, including New York's Carlyle. She was known for her bold combinations, and her finished interiors were often referred to as being "Draperized." (The Stoneleigh Hotel and Spa.)

Harry and Edith Stewart enjoyed traveling and collecting art, and the penthouse became a showcase for their paintings, sculpture, and antique furniture. They sold the Stoneleigh to Leo Corrigan in 1943, and the penthouse was occupied for many years by Wesley Goyer and his wife, Emily, who were active supporters of arts and culture. (The Stoneleigh Hotel and Spa.)

The Stewart penthouse was laid out on two levels, with the bedrooms reached by ascending a short flight of stairs. This not only broke up the long space in the apartment visually but provided a sense of privacy as well. In 2008, the Stoneleigh, including the penthouse, underwent a $36-million renovation. Carleton Varney of Dorothy Draper Company designed the penthouse restoration and transformed the space into a series of event spaces. He used Draper-inspired colors and retained many of Draper's original design elements. (The Stoneleigh Hotel and Spa.)

One of the best views of Dallas was from the rooftop terrace that overlooked the Stoneleigh's gardens. In 1941, radio station KSKY began broadcasting from the 11th floor, and its tagline, "KSKY—atop the beautiful Hotel Stoneleigh overlooking downtown Dallas," became a familiar refrain for listeners. It was an attractive backdrop for television, as seen in this 1955 photograph of actor Jack Webb being interviewed on the terrace for local television, and the hotel was popular with performers who stayed there while performing in town. Texan Margo Jones, noted stage director and actor, called the Stoneleigh home; in 1955, she died after being exposed to fumes from toxic cleaners used to clean the carpet in her apartment. (Left, The Stoneleigh Hotel and Spa; below, Dallas Public Library.)

The Stoneleigh Hotel has hosted dozens of luminaries over the years, many of whom, particularly those in the entertainment business, actually lived at the hotel for a time. In September 1963, Texas governor John Connally and his family posed for *Dallas Times Herald* photographer Andy Hanson at the Stoneleigh just two months before the governor would be seriously wounded during the assassination of President Kennedy. (Author's collection.)

The Melrose Court, at Cedar Springs Road and Oak Lawn Avenue, occupies the site of the George Mellersh home. Mellersh is credited with naming the area Oak Lawn for its natural beauty. Hit hard by the 1893 financial panic, he sold the home, and it was converted to a sheep barn. Banker Ballard Burgher purchased and restored it in 1904 but demolished it in 1924 to develop an apartment hotel. (The Warwick Melrose Dallas.)

THE MELROSE HOTEL — DALLAS, TEXAS

OAKLAWN AT CEDAR SPRINGS   D-4616

The Melrose Court, another Dallas apartment hotel, was designed by C. D. Hill, who came to Texas in 1901 following his education in Chicago. In addition to the Melrose, Hill designed the Oak Lawn Methodist Church and the 1914 city hall. Constructed in the Sullivanesque style, it featured 100 rooms with outside exposures equipped with kitchens for permanent residents. The Melrose operated as an apartment hotel until 1981, when it was purchased by the Banyan Realty Company. Following extensive renovations, it reopened in 1982. The hotel's Bridewell Suite is named for its last permanent resident, whose apartment is pictured below. After a series of owners, it underwent another extensive renovation in 2000 and remains a landmark in the Oak Lawn area. (Both, the Warwick Melrose Dallas.)

Although often considered a Texan, Conrad Hilton was born in New Mexico in 1887, the son of Norwegian immigrants. His father ran a successful general store, but financial losses during a 1907 financial panic forced him to take in boarders, giving Hilton his first experience with the hotel business. After World War I, he purchased his first hotel in Cisco, Texas. Hilton found success in the hotel business with innovative business strategies: leasing and renovating old hotels; building new hotels on leased land; and buying existing hotels cheaply. Between 1925 and 1930, he opened a new Texas hotel every year but nearly went bankrupt during the Depression. He recovered, with the help of investors, but became independent again in 1934. This photograph was taken in 1925, the same year he built his first hotel in Dallas. (Courtesy of the Hospitality Industry Archives, Hilton College/University of Houston.)

Despite being married three times (once to actress Zsa Zsa Gabor), Hilton took his Catholic faith seriously, and in addition to his autobiography published in 1957, he wrote an inspirational book and a prayer, *America on Its Knees*, that was later placed in every Hilton hotel room. After his death in California in January 1979, he was buried in Calvary Hill Cemetery, one of four cemeteries in Dallas owned by the Dallas diocese. The quote on the small headstone (below) refers to his Christmas Day birth date. (Both photographs by Cassie Stewart.)

HILTON HOTEL, DALLAS, TEXAS.

In 1924, in order to preserve capital, Hilton leased the property at the corner of Main and Harwood Streets, which held a brick building occupied by undertakers Loudermilk-Sparkman and began construction of a 14-story hotel—his first high-rise and first to bear the Hilton name. Designed by Dallas architects Lang and Witchell, the reinforced-concrete and masonry Sullivanesque structure was trimmed with terra-cotta and stone. It consisted of a horseshoe plan and had two massive towers facing Harwood Street tied together with an elaborate bridge at the 10th floor. It was completed at a cost of $1,360,000 and opened to the public on August 6, 1925. Hilton marketed the hotel to "The Average Man," believing that Dallas had enough luxury hotels and that clean, moderately priced rooms appealed to businessmen. He maximized space in public areas of the hotel by leasing to contractors who provided rent and offered services such as a pharmacy, barber and beauty shops, a coffee shop, a tailor shop, a telegraph office, and dining rooms. (Author's collection.)

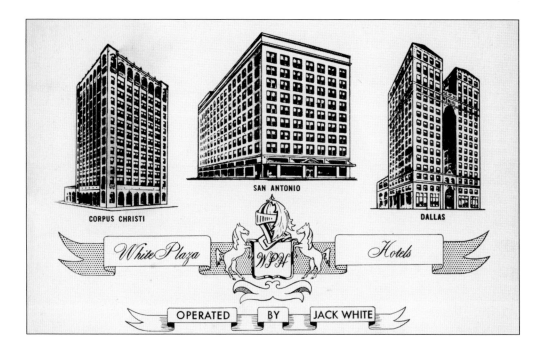

When Hilton relinquished the property lease on the Dallas Hilton Hotel in 1938, George Loudermilk contracted with the hotel's manager, A. C. "Jack" White, who changed its name and formed the White Plaza Company. His company grew, and soon he was operating some of the most prominent hotels in Texas, including the Robert E. Lee and Gunter hotels in San Antonio and the Westbrook and Worth hotels in Fort Worth. He relocated to San Antonio and became involved in local politics and development efforts. (Both, author's collection.)

Though the White Plaza Hotel continued Conrad Hilton's goal of operating a hotel for "The Average Man," certain standards were maintained, such as having a full staff available to assist guests with their needs. This photograph dates from 1950 and shows the hotel's uniformed bellmen standing at attention awaiting their next task. The interior still retains its 1920s appearance, though by 1950, it must have seemed quite dated. (Dallas Public Library.)

The hotel changed hands again in 1974 and was renamed the Plaza. By 1977, many of its floors were closed off until investor Opal Sebastian purchased the hotel in the late 1970s and refurbished the building. After another sale and a 1985 renovation by Corgan Associates, it became the Dallas Plaza Hotel and, a few years later, the Holiday Inn Aristocrat. In 2006, after yet another renovation, it reopened as the Hotel Indigo and remains in business today. (Dallas Heritage Village.)

The Adler Hotel was built sometime in the 1920s on Peak Street near the Texas Baptist Memorial Sanitarium and probably catered to people affiliated with or visiting patients at the hospital, which was renamed Baylor Hospital in 1921. As the area declined, the upper floor was converted to apartments and the lower floor housed a variety of businesses. The building (shown here in 1985), with its sign intact, still stands today. (*The Dallas Morning News*.)

In January 1925, *The Dallas Morning News* illustrated the rapidly changing skyline in a photograph that pictured three hotel projects underway that year: the Baker (2), the Adolphus annex (3), and the Hilton (5). Not shown is the Hotel Scott under construction on Houston Street. The accompanying story said, "The most famous of American city skylines next to that of New York is undergoing a tremendous transformation at the beginning of 1925. (*The Dallas Morning News*.)

AIRPLANE PHOTOGRAPH SHOWS CHANGING CONTOUR OF DALLAS' SKYLINE

—Copyright, Fairchild Aerial Surveys, Inc., Dallas.

This airplane photograph, made a few weeks ago, shows the changing contour of the Dallas skyline at the beginning of 1925. The buildings numbered are: (1) Santa Fe Terminal Office Building, (2) site of eighteen-story Baker Hotel, now being built; (3) Adolphus Hotel Annex, twenty-two stories, under construction; (4) site of Allen Hotel, eighteen-story building to be started this month; (5) fourteen-story Hilton Hotel, under construction; (6) twenty-two-story Republic Bank Building, now under way. No. 7 shows the American Exchange Bank Building, one of the newer skyscrapers. In the center of the picture is the twenty-nine-story Magnolia Petroleum Building, tallest in the South. At the left of this are the Kirby and Praetorian Buildings, earliest of the taller business structures. In the left background is the nineteen-story Medical Arts Building. The Southwestern Life Building is shown between the Magnolia and Kirby Buildings, with the Southland Life to the right of the Magnolia. In the center background, to the right of No. 5, is the Dallas City Hall.

George C. Scott opened the Hotel Scott just days before the Baker's inaugural event. The Scott's debut was low-key, but Jack Gardner's orchestra performed for a live WFAA-Radio broadcast. The Scott was renamed Hotel Lawrence in 1949, and in 1975, Dallas County officials considered purchasing it for use as a jail. In 2000, after changing owners and names several times, it returned to the Hotel Lawrence name and continues to operate today. (Author's photograph.)

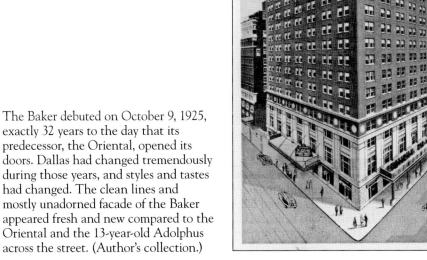

BAKER HOTEL, DALLAS, TEXAS

The Baker debuted on October 9, 1925, exactly 32 years to the day that its predecessor, the Oriental, opened its doors. Dallas had changed tremendously during those years, and styles and tastes had changed. The clean lines and mostly unadorned facade of the Baker appeared fresh and new compared to the Oriental and the 13-year-old Adolphus across the street. (Author's collection.)

The Baker was built by Theodore Brasher Baker (shown here in this 1925 newspaper feature about the hotel's opening), who came to Texas from Kansas sometime around 1918. He built the Texas Hotel in Fort Worth in 1921 and, after opening Dallas's Baker, constructed and operated hotels in Mineral Wells, San Antonio, Austin, and Beaumont. He died in San Antonio in 1972 at the age of 96. (*The Dallas Morning News.*)

Dining options at the Baker included the basement cafeteria, the first in a Dallas hotel, capable of accommodating 400 diners. Decorated with black and white Carrara marble, it was the site of daily musical entertainment. Lawrence Welk and his four-piece band entertained lunchtime diners in the 1930s. Dubbed the "Caveteria," the space was converted to house the Central USO group in 1942 and renamed "The USO Club in the Cave." (Author's collection.)

The Baker's Peacock Terrace debuted with a gala dinner dance in May 1926. The opening night program shown here listed the evening's entertainment and menu. Guests danced to Jimmy Joy's Baker Hotel Orchestra and dined on "Mammy Hannah" fried chicken, fresh peas a la Baker, and "Peacock Salad." (Old Red Museum of Dallas County History and Culture.)

More substantial than Bambooland, the Peacock Terrace was completely enclosed and modeled after an old English inn by Dallas architects Fooshee and Cheek. A contest was held to name the space, and the winner, Baker stenographer Frances Wilson, donated the $50 prize to the Community Chest. Owing to the Texas heat, the Baker's main dining room closed during the summer and meals were served here. (Dallas Heritage Village.)

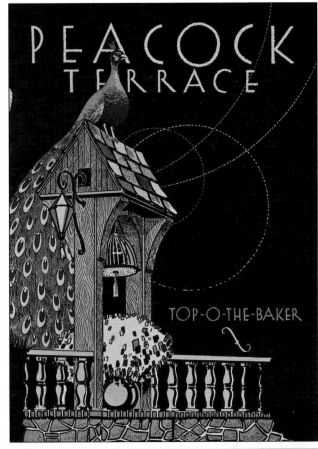

PEACOCK TERRACE, BAKER HOTEL, DALLAS, TEXAS   113583

WFAA, the first network-affiliated radio station in Texas, went on the air in 1922 and broadcast from a tent atop The Dallas Morning News building. In 1925, the Johns Manfield Company designed a modern studio on the Baker's 17th floor that was considered one of the finest in the country. Adjacent to the Peacock Terrace, the station regularly broadcast live orchestra and big band performances as hotel patrons danced to the music. (Author's collection.)

Like the Hilton and the Adolphus, the Baker leased space on its ground floor to florists, jewelry stores, newsstands, liquor stores, and pharmacies that catered to hotel guests as well as downtown workers and shoppers. Marvin's Drug Store was a local chain that opened a branch at the Baker (below), while another Dallas pharmacy, Skillern's, operated a similar establishment at the Adolphus. (Dallas Public Library.)

First Lady Eleanor Roosevelt was honored at a luncheon at the Baker in 1936, while President Roosevelt dined at the Adolphus. Seated at a dais decorated with the six flags of Texas, Joe Betsy Allred, wife of the Texas governor, introduced Mrs. Roosevelt saying, "It is rare and refreshing to find our nation's First Lady more interested in social security and social welfare than in social position." (Author's collection.)

The Baker's elegant Crystal Ballroom was illuminated with six magnificent chandeliers that T. B. Baker imported from Czechoslovakia. In 1953, the first Crystal Charity Ball was held here, and the event took its name from this room. The chandeliers were removed prior to the hotel's demolition in 1980, and two of them were installed in Lee Park's Arlington Hall. (*The Dallas Morning News.*)

The Officers and Directors
of the
Texas Centennial Exposition
request your company at Luncheon
in honor of

Mrs. Franklin Delano Roosevelt

Friday, June the twelfth

One thousand nine hundred thirty-six

twelve o'clock noon

Baker Hotel

Dallas, Texas

Akard Street Canyon
Dallas, Texas

North Akard Street ended where the Baker Hotel stood (seen in the middle of this view). From Jackson Street south, it became South Akard, formerly Sycamore Street. For many years, this was "hotel corner" with the Adolphus standing on the northwest corner of Akard and Commerce Streets (right center of this image). Two AT&T Plaza now occupies the Baker site, and the Magnolia Hotel stands on the northeast corner. (Author's collection.)

After the Japanese surrender ended World War II in August 1945, Dallas celebrated with the rest of the nation. Police braced for the madness as downtown was overrun with joyous throngs of revelers. Businesses closed, officials shuttered liquor stores, and churches held special services. *The Dallas Morning News* reported, "It wasn't long before crowds in the Adolphus and Baker Hotels were ripping pillows apart and dumping feathers into the street." (Dallas Public Library.)

Between 1949 and 1953, the Baker went through a series of improvements. Noted architect George Dahl supervised the projects that added air-conditioning, a drive-up registration area, new elevators, and several expanded and refurbished public rooms for banquets and meetings. This 1950s view, taken from the Adolphus, shows the Adolphus garage in the foreground, and the Statler Hilton, built 1955–1956 can be seen in the distance on the right side of Commerce Street. (Author's collection.)

Large public gatherings were usually held downtown, such as the 1960 ceremony marking the seventh National Day of Prayer. The program was attended by more than 12,000 people, far more than the large hotels could accommodate, so Commerce Street was closed and a flatbed truck served as a stage. Dallas was the country's only major city to consistently observe National Prayer Day since its designation by Congress in 1954. (Dallas Public Library.)

In 1953, the Baker converted the rooftop Peacock Terrace into the Terrace Room, which provided space for nightclub entertainment as well as for dinners and meetings. Designed by George Dahl, the room featured a moveable bandstand and a deep ceiling trimmed in "Mediterranean blue." The walls were paneled in blond oak, and green and gold drapes in a "Monterrey tropical design" covered huge plate-glass windows surrounding the room. (*The Dallas Morning News.*)

Just days before the presidential election in 1960, Texas senator and vice presidential candidate Lyndon Johnson was heckled by supporters of Congressman Bruce Alger, as he and a grim-faced Lady Bird crossed Commerce Street from the Baker to enter the Adolphus for a luncheon. "I'm not bothered," said Johnson. "They're just a bunch of high-school girls." (Lyndon B. Johnson Library and Museum.)

Alexander Sanger was born in Germany in 1847 and followed his older brothers to America in 1865, eventually joining Sanger Brothers, the dry goods business that his brothers had established before his arrival. He settled in Dallas and built a large Victorian mansion on the southwest corner of Ervay and Canton Streets that was described as "one of the show places of the Southwest." Sanger, widely respected for his civic efforts, lived in the home until his death in 1925. His son Elihu leased the site to J. B. Rucker of Rucker and Jones, who demolished the mansion and constructed the Spanish-modern Sanger Hotel and Apartments. The Sanger opened in June 1926 with amenities including telephones in each room, "vanishing" beds, two large porches on the roof, and custom draperies manufactured by Sanger Brothers' suppliers. (Dallas Public Library.)

The National Hotel Company purchased the Sanger in 1948 and renamed it the Hotel Travis. Its solid construction led to its designation as a fallout shelter in the 1950s, but when it was included as part of the site for the new city hall in 1965, it was demolished. Travis manager Ray Little said, "A lot of people are sentimental about this place but not enough to make a monument of the son-of-a-gun." (Dallas Heritage Village.)

Built at a cost of $500,000 by Tucker and McQueen, the Mayfair Hotel faced St. Paul Street between Ross and San Jacinto. Jack Tucker, who opened the hotel in 1927, included a rooftop "Sky Garden" and claimed it was the first of its kind, though the Baker's Peacock Terrace and Bambooland at the Adolphus preceded it. The Sky Garden covered the entire roof, providing a pagoda for dancing and "refreshments and smokes without cost." (Dallas Heritage Village.)

Charles Mangold built the 12-story Cliff Towers on the site of his own home in 1929. He commissioned Chicago architects Hecht and Williams to model the hotel after apartment buildings that he had admired in Italy. Following the national trend of apartment hotels, Cliff Towers accommodated both permanent and transient residents with rooms fitted with closets, kitchens, dinettes, and beds that folded out from the walls. (Author's collection.)

The Cliff Towers was a marvel of technological innovations. Residents' water originated from underground artesian wells and was heated and cooled, and special ventilation systems were installed in the kitchens. Due to the rise of automobile ownership, a 250-car garage, constructed of reinforced concrete and modeled after a typical Italian farmhouse, was added. From 1947 to 1950, radio station KLIF broadcast from its basement studios of the hotel. (Author's collection.)

In 1964, the Cliff Towers (shown here in 1978) was converted to a nursing home and convalescent center, and by the early 1990s, the building was vacant and shuttered. By the turn of the 21st century, the area was experiencing a renaissance, and Evergreen Partners restored the entire building, preserving most of its remaining historic elements, and it reopened as luxury condominiums that provided sweeping views of downtown. (*The Dallas Morning News.*)

An early example of re-purposing downtown buildings was the 1940 conversion of the old North Texas National Bank Building into the 140-room Hotel Maurice. The 1888 structure, originally designed to resemble a fortress, signifying security, was demolished in 1967 to make way for the proposed Two Main Place. This photograph, taken shortly before the building was razed, shows holiday decorations in place on Main Street light poles. (*The Dallas Morning News.*)

D. F. Powell operated the Powell Hotel in the predominately African American State-Thomas area beginning in the 1930s. Its first location was a nondescript, unmarked two-story frame home (above) and later moved to a three-story brick structure (below) located at 3115 State Street. The Powell's guests included Joe Louis, Duke Ellington, Louis Armstrong, and "Fats" Waller. Noted architect William Sidney Pittman lived at the hotel in his later years until his death in 1958. Powell died in 1937, and in the early 1960s, federal anti-discrimination legislation was enacted, rendering hotels such as the Powell unnecessary and archaic. The State-Thomas area declined, and Powell's widow, Ruth, closed the hotel in 1970. Unsuccessful in her attempts to sell the property, the hotel sat vacant and boarded up. A large fire gutted the building in July 1975, and the hotel's burned shell was torn down in 1977. (Both, Dallas Public Library.)

Dallas' Finest and Newest Apartment Hotel

OB-H291

Following World War II, Dallas faced a shortage of housing and hotel rooms. Hotels such as the Highlander Hotel and Apartments at 4217 Lomo Alto Street were built to address these needs. It accommodated both transient and permanent residents. The Imperial Room, a restaurant specializing in continental cuisine, opened at the Highlander in 1949 and was later replaced with the popular Europa restaurant. (Old Red Museum of Dallas County History and Culture.)

In this advertisement, the Chelsea Apartments let African American travelers know that the establishment was welcoming to them. Integrated accommodations were still more than a decade away, and African American visitors often consulted special directories to guide them to "colored hotels." The Chelsea and the Clifton Hotel offered rooms to both long- and short-term tenants. (Author's collection.)

80

Four

ROADSIDE ATTRACTION

Dallas has been busy building tourist camps and tent cities on her outskirts.

—*Time*, June 8, 1936

Hotels, apartments and tourist camps should strive to furnish as many and as attractive rest and sleeping quarters as possible. Dallas has a reputation for hospitality to maintain.

—*The Dallas Morning News*, April 19, 1936

Ned Green reportedly brought the first automobile to Texas in 1899. It arrived in Terrell by train from St. Louis accompanied by its designer George Norris, and the pair took five hours to cover the 30 miles to Dallas. Green formed the first auto club in Dallas in 1903, and a decade later, it boasted 700 members.

Green's club was successful in attracting "national highways" to come through Dallas, and by 1920, four major roads snaked into Dallas. Soon the first tourist courts began to appear, primarily in Oak Cliff near the Bankhead Highway and around Fair Park on Parry and Grand Avenues around the Dixie Overland Highway. Dallas County opened one of the first municipally owned "tourist camps," Camp Simpson, near the fairgrounds. A primitive facility, it provided campsites and crude cabins for the motorist.

Government soon abandoned its tourist camp operations, and entrepreneurs improved upon the concept, building complexes of cottages furnished like tiny homes. As automobile ownership increased, roads connecting Dallas and its neighbors were built, such as Fort Worth Avenue, location of many motor hotels or "motels."

Rarely were local leaders out of touch in regard to Dallas's accommodations, but the centennial celebrations in 1936 illustrated the importance in planning for a large influx of visitors. Construction of new rooms was impressive but inadequate to host a world's fair, leading officials to plead with citizens to open private homes to accommodate visitors and to create tent cities to house the overflow.

After the war, the motel business exploded with automobile ownership but began to decline in the late 1960s and 1970s as interstate highways bypassed Dallas's urban core. The term "motel" largely fell out of favor, and today national chains operate most of these establishments, rendering hotels and motels largely indistinguishable.

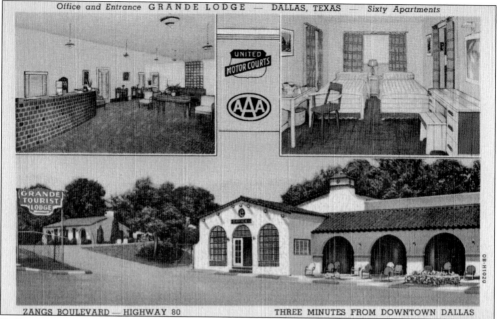

Dallas attorney Marcus Plowman opened the Grande Tourist Lodge in 1929. Designed by architects Fooshee and Cheek, the Spanish Colonial–style motel was built on a lush site on Zang Boulevard near the Houston Street viaduct. Plowman expanded his business into other Texas cities until his death in 1944. (Dallas Heritage Village.)

The Grande Tourist Lodge was considered one of the finest of Dallas's early roadside motels. Comprised of 60 bungalow-styled apartments, Grande Lodge interiors were furnished and decorated to resemble typical living rooms of the day and offered telephones and private bathrooms. The gated entry conveyed a sense of security, and its design influenced other similar Dallas establishments. The motel was demolished in 1994. (Dallas Heritage Village.)

"One of Dallas' Newest and Finest Motels"

The Texas Motel was typical of the motels and tourist courts that sprang up in the late 1920s and early 1930s. Motel operators attempted to stand out with distinctive architecture, clean properties, and eye-catching roadside signs, like the Texas's neon cactus. As of August 2009, the Texas Motel property still stands at 3816 West Davis Street in Oak Cliff. (Author's collection.)

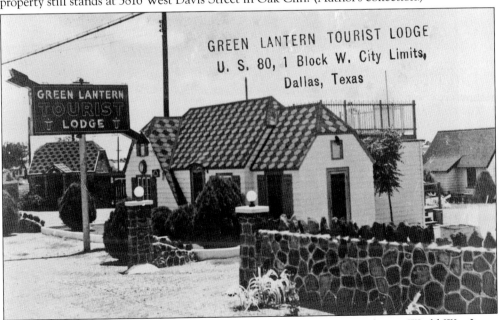

Marie Henslee was born in Dallas and moved to Washington, D.C., during World War I as a civilian military worker. Returning to Dallas, she and her husband, George, operated the Green Lantern Tourist Lodge for several years. Her father, Gustave Santerre, was born in the La Reunion colony in 1857, and her mother, Rosa, in a home where the Dallas County Records building now stands. (Dallas Heritage Village.)

The New Westerner Tourist Courts

2514 SOUTH ZANGS BLVD. AT ELMORE STREET
U. S. HIGHWAY 67 AND 77 SOUTH - DALLAS, TEXAS
PHONE MADISON 8000

Location was vital to the success of tourist courts and motels. The New Westerner Tourist Courts, located at 2514 South Zang Boulevard, was built adjacent to the busy intersection of U.S. Highway 67 and Highway 77 South. Both highways were merged into R. L. Thornton Freeway as part of the Federal Highway Act of 1956. The New Westerner still operates as the Carefree Inn. (Author's collection.)

The motel and tourist court business was highly competitive, and owners of these establishments employed a variety of marketing gimmicks to entice potential customers to pull off of the road. Fanciful architecture and bright neon signs were traditional means of drawing in guests. Exotic sounding names such as "La Tourista Courts" were used, despite the fact that the motel itself resembled a typical American neighborhood. (Author's collection.)

84

The Bon Air Courts was located at 3811 Ross Avenue and was typical of the many tourist courts built to accommodate visitors to the 1936 Texas Centennial Exposition. Consisting of 25 cabins, the motel was built for $10,000. The construction boom, coupled with federal funds for WPA projects, boosted the total amount of Dallas construction permits in the first four months of 1936 to nearly $4 million. (Dallas Heritage Village.)

Jabe and Leora Gibson came to Dallas from Nebraska in 1931. After his arrival, Jabe Gibson established one of the first travel bureaus in the country. His wife founded Gibson Hotels, and she owned and operated several Dallas motels for more than 27 years, including Carson Manor, the Plaza Hotel, and the Rivera Courts on Fort Worth Avenue. (Author's collection.)

The family road trip posed unexpected adventures, particularly where development encroached on nature. Newspaper reports in 1955 told of the Pingrey family of Seattle, who after checking into the Shamrock on Buckner Boulevard discovered that a skunk had entered their cabin as they unloaded their car. A two-hour standoff ensued, and eventually the skunk was removed after animal control officers fed the creature hamburger laced with sleeping pills. (Dallas Heritage Village.)

Automobile travelers, especially those with children, often found roadside accommodations unpredictable in cleanliness and security. Membership in organizations such as the American Automobile Association, Master Host, and Quality Courts assured customers that a motel met their high standards. By 1962, over half of the nation's motels, such as the El Sombrero on Harry Hines, belonged to such groups. (Dallas Heritage Village.)

ALAMO PLAZA HOTEL COURTS

AMERICA'S FINEST

BATON ROUGE, SHREVEPORT AND NEW ORLEANS, LA.   ATLANTA, GA.   LITTLE ROCK, ARKANSAS

MEMPHIS AND NASHVILLE, TENN.   OKLAHOMA CITY, OKLA.   CHARLOTTE AND RALEIGH, N. C.

BEAUMONT, DALLAS, HOUSTON, TYLER AND WACO, TEXAS   GULFPORT AND JACKSON, MISS.

Lee Torrance and Drummond Bartlett opened the Alamo Plaza Tourist Apartments in Waco in 1929. Shortly after, the pair dissolved the partnership, and Torrance built another Alamo Plaza in Tyler in 1931. It proved successful, and Torrance began building Alamo Plazas in cities across the South, making it one of the country's first motel chains. Many of Torrance's innovations, such as placing telephones in rooms, were copied by other motels. Others used the Alamo Plaza name, and the Dallas property was opened about 1940 on Fort Worth Avenue by Dallas businessmen Charles Mooney and Bill Farner, who owned 10 Alamo Plazas. The 1960s saw the area decline, and in 1976, Indian immigrants Chandrakant and Surekha Patel purchased the Alamo Plaza (shown below in 1980) and became successful innkeepers, eventually owning more than two-dozen local motels. (Above, Dallas Heritage Village; below, *The Dallas Morning News*.)

Jim Crow laws segregated blacks and whites in public places such as stores, theaters, and hotels. African American visitors to Dallas needed places to stay, but there were only a handful of hotels to accommodate them, and they were forced to choose from them, stay in private homes, or sleep in their cars. Frank Grant Jr. managed the Ross Avenue Motel from 1959 to 1971. (Dallas Heritage Village.)

Lee Montgomery was a Kentucky native who came to Dallas in the 1930s and made a career of managing hotels in the area. He operated the Clifton Hotel and Apartments on West Colorado for many years before managing the Carlton Motel until his retirement. He died in Dallas in 1965. (Author's collection.)

Belmont Motor Hotel

THE HOTEL WITH THE SKY-VIEW OF DALLAS

The Belmont Motor Hotel at 905 Fort Worth Avenue opened in June 1942 with a live radio broadcast on WFAA. Designed by Charles Dilbeck, the California-styled motel offered 75 rooms on a 5-acre bluff providing panoramic views of the city. Newspapers reported at the Belmont's opening, "Elevation of the several units range from thirty-five feet to fifty feet above the highway, affording an unusual view of the Dallas business district skyline." An adjacent restaurant featured three named dining rooms, the Mobile, Dallas, and Cosmopolitan, and a mobile sculpture by John Donald Popejay hung from the ceiling. Like many of its neighbors, the Belmont declined along with the neighborhood until Monte Anderson bought and lovingly restored the Belmont (renamed the Belmont Hotel) in 2005. (Both, Dallas Heritage Village.)

THE *Belmont* MOTOR HOTEL
DALLAS

In the 1940s and 1950s, West Davis Street between Westmoreland and Cockrell Hill Roads was dotted with motels and cafés that appealed to the motorist. Visitors to the Ritz Motel need not look far for entertainment diversions as it was located across from the Chalk Hill Drive-In Theater. Many of these motels can still be seen today in the areas around Fort Worth Avenue and Davis Street. (Dallas Heritage Village.)

William Hammond opened the Laurel Lodge Hotel Courts at 5545 South Beckley in June 1951, with an open house where women were presented with "orchids flown from Hawaii," children with ice cream and balloons, and men with "a variety of souvenirs." Twenty-seven of the sixty rooms were configured as efficiency apartments, and a motel-owned station wagon served as a courtesy car for guests. (Author's collection.)

The Crestpark Apartment Hotel at Lomo Alto and Gilbert Streets was completed in 1952. The nine-story building operated as a 192-unit complex offering furnished and unfurnished apartments. Its location adjacent to Highland Park made it popular with prominent Dallas retirees including jeweler Clifton Linz and department store executive Leon Harris Jr. Bandleader and composer Hoagy Carmichael was a guest of the Crestpark in 1953 while headlining the Crystal Charity Ball that year. (Dallas Heritage Village.)

The Roma Motel located near Lovers Lane on Greenville Avenue opened in the late 1950s and was the site of a tragic crime after desk clerk George Hooper was kidnapped and killed on New Year's Day 1968. Donald Mitchell was sentenced to life in prison for the crime seven years later. Following another murder there in 1973, the motel was razed when Old Town Center was built. (Author's collection.)

After the Dallas Trade Mart was established along the Stemmons corridor in 1958, new hotels and motels soon followed. In 1960, Dallas architect Harold Berry designed the Marriott Motor Hotel in a western ranch design opposite Stemmons Freeway from the Merchandise Mart. Richard Nixon visited the hotel twice in 1968 while seeking the Republican presidential nomination and again as president in 1970 before delivering an address at Market Hall. (Author's collection.)

The Holiday Terrace Motel was built in 1960 by developers Joe Nevins, T. C. Strickland, and L. A. Fonville for $135,000. The motel contained 50 rooms and featured free television, a children's playground, and the Golden Ox restaurant. Although the swimming pool and playground are gone, the motel continues to operate as the Astro Inn. (Author's collection.)

The NorthPark Inn, located on Central Expressway just north of Park Lane, opened in November 1963, two years before the opening of NorthPark Center. Owner/developer W. W. Caruth Jr. expanded the luxury motel three times within five years of its opening. Although the area was developing rapidly, the location was still remote enough that management boasted "two riding stables and small lakes for fishing are located nearby." (Author's collection.)

National chain hostelries such as Holiday Inn standardized motel architecture and function and followed the development of new highways and roads. The Holiday Inn North, located at the huge interchange of Central Expressway and LBJ Freeway, opened on the site of a former nursery in 1968. Holiday Inn executives constructed the hotel there when it was predicted that by 1970 "170,000 cars will be passing the intersection daily." (Author's collection.)

After World War II, most middle-class families owned at least one car and family road trips became popular summer rituals. Tourist courts of the 1920s and 1930s seemed dated, run-down, and often dangerous—not desirable qualities for families traveling with children. New suburban hotels like Leo Corrigan's Lynn and Lakewood Hotels in East Dallas were built with families in mind and often included playgrounds and swimming pools. *Hotel Monthly*, an industry publication, reported that hotels that added a swimming pool saw their business increase by as much as 60 percent, and some hotel associations actually required member hotels to have pools. Though labeled "hotels," these properties melded characteristics of hotels and motels, and the distinctions between the two began to blur. (Both, Dallas Heritage Village.)

Five

WAKE-UP CALL

Dallas is the national focal point and new hotels will invite even larger conventions.

—Ernest Henderson Sr., president of Sheraton Corporation of America, 1955

This could well mark the end of an era.

—Marilyn Schwartz on the opening of the Rosewood Crescent Courts, 1986

After the war, city leaders knew the time was right for another large hotel downtown, as a generation had passed since the Baker opened its doors. Convention business was on the rise, and Dallas actively pursued plans to develop and build a new convention hotel. Once again, local investors stepped up to the plate and raised over $1 million to attract the Statler Hotel, which opened in 1956. Development of the sprawling Southland Center in 1959 heralded the opening of the 600-room Sheraton Hotel. A decade later, the Fairmont Hotel debuted, and it, along with the Statler, brought in first-rate entertainment rarely seen outside of New York and Las Vegas.

The city's demographics began to change, and in the 1960s and 1970s, rapid growth of surrounding communities saw large numbers of residents and businesses retreat farther away from the city center. The phrase "urban renewal" entered the lexicon, and historic hotels such as the Jefferson, the Baker, the Southland, the Sanger, and the last traces of the St. George were demolished in the name of progress. Plans for a Frank Lloyd Wright–designed hotel, the Rogers Lacy, never materialized.

The situation was not entirely grim. In 1978, Hyatt opened a 1,000-room hotel near Union Station. The complex included the 560-foot Reunion Tower, giving the skyline its most distinctive landmark and new symbol of the city when it figured prominently in the opening credits of the popular television series *Dallas*, which premiered that year. The Anatole opened the following year and attracted Dallas's first national political convention in 1984. Dallas-based Rosewood Corporation opened its mansard-topped Crescent Court in 1986, spawning development in the State-Thomas/McKinney Avenue area.

Dallas was once again moving forward, but the situation turned bleak with the onset of the oil bust of the mid-1980s, when the price of Texas crude plummeted, devastating the city and state's economy and grinding to a halt most new construction. As the economy declined, several iconic hotels became ripe for acquisition by overseas investors, including the Stoneleigh, Melrose, and Fairmont.

4 Convenient SUBURBAN LOCATIONS IN DALLAS

LOMA ALTO HOTEL 4518 Lemmon Ave.

Convenient to all major highways, out of downtown traffic congestion. Free parking adjoining. AAA-approved. Summer-Winter air conditioned, all rooms with bath and circulating ice water. Coffee Shop, "Flight Room" for meetings and banquets. Less than five minutes from Love Field. Charles A. Closson, Mgr.

Telephone LAkeside 2174

LAWN HOTEL 3718 Lemmon Ave.

In the Oak Lawn District. Convenient to all major highways, yet out of downtown traffic congestion. Free parking adjoining. Summer-Winter air conditioned, all rooms with bath and circulating ice water. Radio in every room. Curtis L. Wells, Resident Manager.

Telephone LOgan 6684

LAKEWOOD HOTEL 1818 Abrams Rd.

In the Lakewood Shopping District. Convenient to all major highways, out of downtown traffic congestion. Free parking adjoining. Summer-Winter air conditioned, all rooms with bath and circulating ice water. Ben F. Cumnock, Resident Manager.

Telephone VIctor 1601

LYNN HOTEL 3405 Gaston Ave.

Across the street from Baylor Hospital. Convenient to all major highways, near downtown Dallas. Free parking adjoining. Summer-Winter air conditioned, all rooms with combination tub and shower bath, circulating ice water. Coffee Shop. Henry E. Boren, Manager.

Telephone VIctor 6331

Affiliated with the new **air conditioned Loring Hotel**, Camp Bowie Blvd. and University Dr., **Fort Worth, Texas**. Telephone: EDison 1291. John W. McCann, Mgr.

In 1949, the Dallas Chamber of Commerce commissioned Hockenbury System, Inc., to determine Dallas's hotel needs. The firm's survey showed a definite need for a major hotel addition. Dallas was not alone. Shortages of materials and labor during the war years had left many major cities deficient in hotel room numbers in addition to shortages in housing for returning veterans who were starting careers and families. Dallas investor Leo Corrigan saw the city's need and the economic opportunity, purchased his first hotel in 1943, and continued to expand his real estate investment company, which, by 1955, included hotels, office buildings, and shopping centers. He owned the Stoneleigh for a time and developed and operated Dallas's Lomo Alto, Lakewood, Lawn, and Lynn Hotels. (Author's collection.)

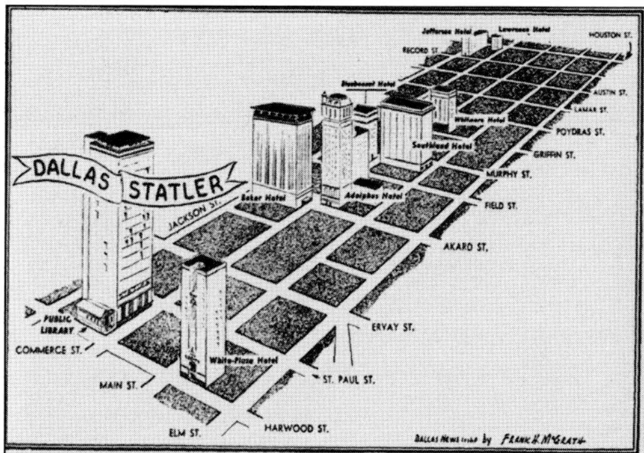

Site selected for the proposed $10,000,000 Dallas Hotel Statler, consisting of most of the 1900 block of Commerce with the exception of the Dallas Public Library property, is shown above in its relation to other principal ntown hotels. The representation of the new Statle: is purely imaginary, no plans or designs having been drawn as yet for the structure.

Commerce Site Picked For New Statler Hotel

By DON MacIVER
Business Editor of The News

On a site adjoining the Dallas Public Library in the 1900 block of Commerce, construction will start early next spring for a $10,000,000 Hotel Statler of 750 to 800 rooms.

Selection of the site was announced from New York Saturday by Arthur F. Douglas, president of Hotels Statler Co., Inc.

The hotel will front 307 feet on Commerce and 195 feet on Jackson and will occupy most of the block except for the library property.

The block is bounded on the east by St. Paul and on the west by Harwood. The hotel will face north, its entrance on Commerce.

Cost of the site will be more than $1,000,000, it was announced by J. N. Fisher, realtor, who has obtained options on the property as trustee for the account of the Statler company. The company expects to take title before Oct. 1, Douglas said.

"The hotel will be one of the finest in the United States and certainly the finest in the South and Southwest," the Statler president declared.

"Hotels Statler Co., Inc., is going ahead with the contract and agreement which it signed with Cosmopolitan Hotels of Dallas, Inc., which will provide capital, in part, for the new hotel."

The Cosmopolitan Hotel corporation was formed by a group of Dallas business leaders to work with Statler in building the new hotel. Its agreement calls for raising $1,500,000 in Dallas as a loan to the Statler company to help finance the enterprise.

Officers of the Dallas corporation are Fred F. Florence, president; R. L. Thornton, vice-president, and Stanley Marcus, secretary.

The Statler company will provide the additional $8,500,000 required to finance the $10,000,000 project.

Douglas said his company soon hopes to have architectural plans for the hotel and quickly thereafter will announce the selection of the contractor and Dallas architect. These plans will be drawn by the Statler company's staff architect who will be associated with the Dallas architect in making the final design and specifications.

Fisher said Statler's plans call for the hotel to have a solid frontage extending 307 feet on Commerce Street, with dining rooms and banquet rooms at the rear of the plot. Height of the building has not been determined, he added.

To acquire the 50,000-square-foot site, Fisher said he had to purchase other property in the vicinity to exchange for certain sections of the plot. Some of New York's finer shops have already applied for space along Commerce Street, Fisher added.

The site embraces the full block except for the 100x200-foot library property and two small plots, one of 100x62 feet at the corner of St. Paul and Jackson and the other of 100x50 feet adjoining the library and fronting on Jackson. The location was approved by J. J. Chambers, Atlanta, La., Statler's real estate consultant.

Douglas stressed in his announcement, that the new hotel will be completely air conditioned and would have full convention and banquet facilities.

Generally considered the nation's top hotel chain, Statler Hotels now are operating in eight cities—New York, Boston, Buffalo, Cleveland, Detroit, St. Louis, Washington and Pittsburgh. All bear the Statler name except the Hotel William Penn in Pittsburgh.

The New York Statler was formerly the Hotel Pennsylvania.

Ground was broken July 5 for a $20,000,000 Statler hotel-office building in Los Angeles which will extend the chain to the West Coast.

The Dallas Statler will be tenth in the chain.

The chain was founded in the early years of this century by Ellsworth Milton Statler, who has been called the "inventor" of the modern American hotel. He created the design and pattern of the modern hotel with his first hotel in Buffalo in 1907, then went on to pioneer many improvements in design, construction and service as he added new hotels to his holdings. Statler died in 1928.

His policy that "the guest is always right" has been the watchword for Statler operating policies ever since.

The present operating head of the chain, President Arthur F. Douglas, has expressed himself as bullish about the outlook for the hotel industry.

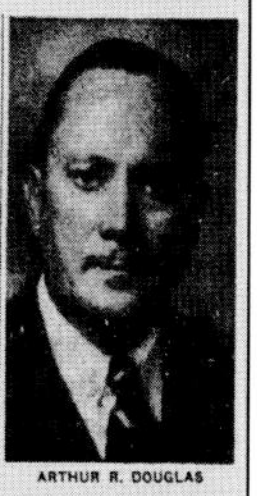

ARTHUR R. DOUGLAS

"My own feeling is that the outlook in the foreseeable future is good," he recently declared.

"I believe that the basic factors responsible for the improvement in our business just prior to the war are still present and will continue to be felt. That is to say, I believe travel will continue to be reasonably high; and that there will not be an oversupply of hotel accommodations in most of our cities. The law of supply and demand will function, I believe, to our advantage."

The Hockenbury study recommended a 500-room luxury hotel for downtown Dallas. In 1950, the chamber of commerce formed a committee to explore the feasibility of constructing such a facility. Executives with the Statler and Sheraton hotel chains expressed interest in the project, but in the end, a bid by Statler to build an 800-room hotel was given the nod. The Statler proposal, much like the negotiations between local officials and Adolphus Busch 40 years earlier, called for the city to raise capital for the project, offering to construct the hotel with Statler funds but with a $1.5-million loan from local backers. No public money was involved. Business leaders, headed by banker Fred Florence, formed the Cosmopolitan Hotel Company to raise the funds, and by the end of 1950, the site had been selected and initial design work had been completed. (Both, *The Dallas Morning News.*)

STATLER ACTION

Spring Beginning Set for New Hotel

By June, third anniversary of the announcement that Hotels Statler Company, Inc., would build here, the hotel may be well under construction.

After months of work on plans and postponement of construction's beginning, it appeared Saturday that work of excavating the site would start in March.

It will take two years.

Arthur F. Douglas, the company's president, told The Dallas News plans finally should be finished around Feb. 1. Then they would be submitted to contractors.

"The early spring," Douglas said, "would be a good time to start construction in Dallas."

As every projected completion date for the plans passed without their completion, some sentiment grew in Dallas that the hotel might not be built. The Statler, some persons speculated, would find construction costs prohibitive and back out.

Douglas, however, insisted all the time he would build.

Part of the delay in finishing of architects' plans apparently was caused by changes in plans, part by waiting to see what the City Council would do with the Dallas public library's adjoining site. One of the changes in plans will be to increase the public space on the ground floor.

J. N. Fisher, Statler leasing agent here, said he had been besieged by firms wanting to lease ground-floor space for high-class shops, transportation ticket offices and places like that.

Contractors will be asked to bid on a 1,001-room hotel, air-conditioned throughout. Original plans

See STATLER, Page 8, Col. 1.

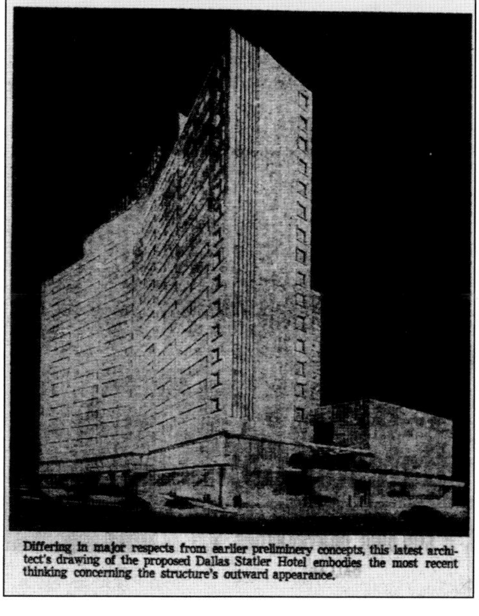

Differing in major respects from earlier preliminery concepts, this latest architect's drawing of the proposed Dallas Statler Hotel embodies the most recent thinking concerning the structure's outward appearance.

BAN ON NEW BUILDINGS IMPERILS STATLER HOTEL

The government Monday abruptly halted construction of commercial buildings to save defense materials.

Dallas' long-sought Statler Hotel can be built now only if federal permission is obtained, and millions of dollars' worth of other construction in Dallas may be delayed, if not blocked entirely.

The order stops for thirty days, construction of new stores, hotels, and other commercial buildings. It paves the way for a strict federal licensing system which will go into effect Feb. 15.

At that time, builders who wish to put up banks, barbershops, restaurants, shoe repair shops or mortuaries will have to show that they are essential for defense, health, welfare or safety.

Arthur Douglas, president of Statler Hotels, could not be reached for comment on the ban. He has repeatedly said he believes a new hotel to be a "necessity" for Dallas.

The ban doesn't automatically shut down all construction now going on. A project already started will be exempt. The catch is in the definition of "started."

Fred Florence, president of the Republic National Bank, which has been working for months on a plan for a huge new office building, said he did not "think of the ban as applying to buildings such as ours."

For Republic's new building, Florence said, construction is already under way, materials have been purchased and committed excavation work is going on and the steel 1 s been bought and is in fabrication.

As for the Statler, said Florence, who was instrumental in interesting Statler officials in building here, it might be necessary to go to the government and present a case for the Statler as necessary construction here.

Statler President Douglas has often pointed out that he finished the Washington Statler during World War II on the grounds that Washington needed it. He has said he thinks he can do the same thing here.

In this connection, Clifton Blackmon, publicity chief of the Dallas Chamber of Commerce, said that a survey of office space here is now under way.

It will list space available now and estimate the space needed for a city named one of fifteen "defense capitals" in the nation, a designation Dallas already has.

Blackmon and some builders here thought such a survey might show that many of the projects planned for Dallas are urgent.

Meanwhile, some projects seemed immune from the ban. The enlargement of Hotel Adolphus, already well under way, seemed certain to be exempt. So did the new Neiman-Marcus store in Preston Center.

Edwin B. Jordan of Leo Corrigan's office, said he hoped the new Corrigan Tower has been "started" under terms of the act. Demolition work has been going on since Dec. 1 and the building permit was secured then. But a foundation has not actually been laid.

In Grand Prairie, where the Corrigan interests project a new hotel and shopping center, the site is already under preparation, Jordan said.

"But we just won't know where we stand until we see the whole order," Jordan said. "I certainly hope we can go ahead."

The same comment, in effect came from Edward S. Marcus, executive vice-president of Neiman Marcus, which has announced a huge enlargement program for the downtown store. Work started on the project on the first of the year.

"But until we see the order, we just don't know where we stand," Marcus said. "The next forty-eight hours ought to clear things up."

The clampdown on commercial building follows a ban on almost all forms of new buildings for recreation and amusement, such as dance halls, motion picture theaters and bowling alleys. Both moves are designed to save steel copper and other scarce material needed for defense production and buildings.

Plans for the Statler appeared to move ahead quickly, but in 1951, the project encountered a series of delays. In January, the federal government's National Production Authority issued a ban on new commercial construction to conserve building materials, a result of the United States's entry into the Korean conflict and to cold war–era sensibilities. By summer, Dallas's funds had been committed, and the project received NPA approval to move ahead, but a national steel shortage slowed further progress. When it appeared that these issues had been resolved, a local issue added another delay: Statler builders hoped to acquire the entire block of land between Commerce, Jackson, Harwood, and St. Paul Streets, a site that included Dallas's 1901 Carnegie library building. It was clear that the cramped facility should be replaced, but debate over a location for a new library dragged on. (Both, *The Dallas Morning News.*)

—Dallas News Staff Photo

URGES THIRD LIBRARY SITE

Realtor Lawrence Miller, at the microphone before the City Council Monday, injected a new note in the library location squabble. He suggested the city should buy most of the block across Harwood from City Hall, build a library with a park in front and underground parking. Back to the camera is Councilman J. R. Terry.

Pressure Rises In Library Tiff

By ALLEN QUINN

Contending forces in the library location controversy piled new pressure on the City Council Monday. And the situation grew more confused than ever.

The mounting confusion was heightened by these developments:

1. Library Board President Boude Storey Sr. reported an offer of $300,000 by unidentified Dallas interests for the old Harwood-Commerce library site where it has been planned to build a new library. That topped—by $100,000—the offer of Hotels Statler Company, Inc., and threw a monkey wrench into the plans of those plugging for sale to Statler.

2. About sixty persons, led by John W. Carpenter, appeared at the Council session and a dozen of them argued for selling to Statler and building the new library on the auditorium site west of Akard and south of Marilla. Left alone to argue for building on the old site was J. F. Hyman, chairman of the board of directors of the Friends of the Public Library.

3. Realtor Lawrence Miller renewed a suggestion made several months ago that eastern two thirds of the block across Harwood from City Hall be bought. It would make a beautiful library site with a park in front, he said.

4. Chester L. Lance, who led the fight which resulted in dropping plans for a civic center, opposed moving the library to the auditorium site. He called it a scheme to revive the civic center plan.

5. It became apparent that a majority of Councilmen now favor a new site for the library, but not on the auditorium tract.

6. Councilman W. C. Miller drew from Hyman a statement that Friends of the Library probably could raise money by popular subscription to make up the difference in cost of a new site and what the old one would bring.

The Councilmen took no action on the library question. It was indicated they would wait to get details on the offer reported by Storey.

The library president did not attend the Council session.

"We have a definite and unsolicited offer of $300,000, which would permit the library to remain where it is, rent free, until a new building is built." Storey said.

Storey said he was not at liberty to say who made the offer.

"It was made by Dallas citizens and not the Statler," he said.

Asked if the offer would be made formally to the Council, Storey said: "I am sure it will be made in time; it depends on the attitude of the Council on the library location."

Councilmen said, informally, there was no question of accepting the Statler offer with a $500,000 offer reported. It brought up the possibility that if the Council decided the new library should be on another site, the library should be so anchored.

See LIBRARY, Page 2, Co. 2

The city council, under public pressure, voted to build the library where the 1901 Carnegie building stood. Critics said that the Statler would make it "look like a lean-to" and that the new building "would prevent the Statler from being as attractive as it would be with the entire block." In September 1955, four months before the Statler was completed, the George Dahl–designed Central Library opened. (Author's collection.)

Hotel Statler-Hilton
Dallas, Texas

Construction began in 1953, and in late 1954, Conrad Hilton acquired controlling interest in Hotels Statler, Inc., but said that the move would have no effect on the hotel's completion. The only change would be the hotel's name: it would be called the Statler Hilton instead of the Hotel Statler. This postcard shows a rendering of the hotel with "Statler Hotel" across the top of the building, a sign that never existed. (Author's collection.)

THE STATLER HILTON
DALLAS, TEXAS
WILLIAM B. TABLER, Architect
September 1, 1955   ROBERT E. McKEE, General Contractor, Inc.

By September 1955, exterior work was nearly complete. Designed by New York's William B. Tabler, the postmodern, 19-story building was the first in the world to make full use of flat-slab, cantilever construction that eliminated many of the footings and columns found in older construction. The exterior was composed of porcelain-coated steel produced by Dallas-based Texlite, Inc., prompting many to nickname the Statler Hilton the "Porcelain Palace." It was said that the hotel contained more innovations than any other hotel in the country. Besides the unique architecture, it boasted "exhibitors panels" with hidden electrical outlets for trade shows, a hoist for lifting automobiles into the ballroom, a heliport, and piped-in music in the elevators. Each of the 1,001 rooms contained combination television/radios and Servidors—hollow room doors that held guests' shoes or laundry for easy access by hotel maids. (Hospitality Industry Archives, Hilton College/ University of Houston.)

Conrad Hilton and Alice Statler attended a star-studded party to celebrate the opening of the hotel in January 1956, despite miserable weather. Celebrities and movie stars arrived at Love Field on two special charter planes where they were greeted by Hilton and Dallas mayor R. L. Thornton. Piper Laurie, Hedda Hopper, Ann Miller, and Dorothy Malone were among the celebrities to deplane and board surreys, buggies, and vintage automobiles for the ride across the tarmac to a hospitality tent. From Love Field, guests were driven downtown. Festivities included public appearances by the stars, elaborate banquets, and musical entertainment. Thornton remarked that the Statler Hilton "will make Dallas one of the top four or five convention cities in the nation." (Above, Hospitality Industry Archives, Hilton College/University of Houston; right, *The Dallas Morning News*.)

Stars Arrive For Hotel Fete

By FRANCIS RAFFETTO

NOTABLES HERE FOR GALA EVENT
Two planeloads of Hollywood stars and other national figures caused a swirl of activity as they landed at Southwest Airmotive Sunday to begin launching the new Statler Hilton Hotel in Dallas. Left foreground is Virginia Warren, daughter of Chief Justice Earl Warren and right foreground is Jerome Zerbe, magazine photographer. Conrad N. Hilton stands to the left of Mayor R. L. Thornton. Charles Meeker of the State Fair of Texas looks off to the left of the picture; Hollywood's Ann Miller is in the left background, and Singer Margaret Whiting is at extreme right.

SINGER IN A SURREY
Lisa Kirk, who appeared last in Dallas in "Kiss Me Kate," was one of the Hollywood stars who were greeted by Dallas officials, and old-time buggies and cars as they landed in Dallas for the Statler Hilton festivities. She was amused by this 100-year-old surrey without the fringe on top.

101

in Dallas The

Statler Hilton

Located in the heart of downtown Dallas, the new Statler Hilton has been designed with just one thought in mind — the comfort of its guests. The 21-floor, Y-shaped building is completely air conditioned from the smart lobby to deluxe Skyline Suites. Quiet, luxurious comfort keynotes 1,001 handsomely furnished guest rooms — and each looks out across a brilliant panorama of Dallas through broad picture windows. Fourteen dining rooms provide every type of food from a quick snack to the most exotic cuisine. There is the fine Empire Room, with America's top supper club entertainers, the Embassy Ballroom and the Grand Ballroom, largest in the South. Out past the lobby the serene picture pool and flashing modern sculpture grace the patio. In a word, every feature of The Statler Hilton is planned to cater to your comfort at this great new hotel where hospitality is a treasured and gracious art.

Specially designed to handle large groups smoothly, and backed by a world-famous reputation for hospitality, and wonderful service, The Statler Hilton is one of the nation's outstanding sites for group gathering and conventions.

The glamorous Grand Ballroom — The South's largest

Hilton Hotels
Conrad N. Hilton, President

DALLAS • JUNE, 1958   49

This advertisement ran in the local chamber of commerce's magazine, *Dallas*. The hotel's modern features such as its choice of fine food, modern sculpture, air-conditioning, and sleek design featured prominently in both the copy and illustrations. The advertisement promotes the Statler Hilton's convention facilities, including its ballrooms promoted as "the largest in the South." The ballrooms were flexible space and could be combined to accommodate more than 2,000 people at a single gathering. The floor plan indicates the locations of the hotel's public rooms. The Empire Room, the hotel's main restaurant and nightclub, featured a dance floor that could be hydraulically raised for performances and lowered below floor level to provide space for an ice rink. (Left, author's collection; below, *The Dallas Morning News*.)

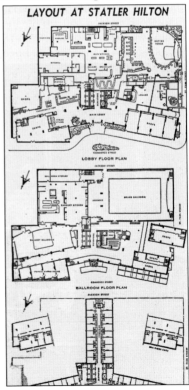

Statler guests had an array of dining options. This menu for the hotel's "Coffee House and Grill" offered casual fare while the Empire Room offerings were more upscale in fitting with its supper club atmosphere. In addition, there was a third restaurant as well as an employee cafeteria. The Grill's space could be added to the Empire Room's to make it the largest nightclub in Dallas. (Author's collection.)

The 1959 Neiman Marcus fortnight focused on South America and brought high-profile visitors to the city. Llinda Llee Llama, who added an Andean flavor to the event, stayed in a special suite at the Statler Hilton. Newspapers reported that after checking in with manager Joseph Cavaghnarro, Llinda Llee promptly licked the glue from an envelope she had been handed while skeptical housekeeping staff looked on. (Dallas Public Library.)

In 1988, Hilton Hotels sold the Statler to overseas investors, who operated it as the Dallas Grand Hotel. It closed in 2001, and although there has been talk of reopening it as either a hotel or condominiums, no plans have materialized. The future of the building remains unclear. In 2008, it was included on the National Trust for Historic Preservation's list of "America's Most Endangered Places." (Author's collection.)

The Executive Inn, located on Mockingbird Lane across from Love Field, opened in 1961, providing convenient accommodations for air travelers, a modern version of the early hotels that were constructed around Union Station downtown. The postmodern, six-story hotel with its sawtooth drive-up entrance, was home to the Empire Room, an intimate cabaret that presented live entertainment by singers, comedians, and variety acts. (*The Dallas Morning News.*)

Dallas-based Southland Life, one of the nation's largest life insurance companies, announced plans in 1954 to construct a complex covering the block between Live Oak, Bryan, Olive, and Pearl Streets. Southland Center consisted of a 50-story headquarters building for Southland Life, which when completed was the tallest building west of the Mississippi, and a 28-story, 600-room Sheraton Hotel. Another tower was added in 1980. Outside of Las Vegas and Florida, there had been just six major hotels projects built in the United States since 1942. With the Statler-Hilton and the Sheraton, Dallas would claim two, effectively solving its hotel room deficit. By late 1957, the hotel tower was complete enough to allow Sheraton officials to raise its corporate flag to the top of the steel framework. (Right, Old Red Museum of Dallas County History and Culture; below, *The Dallas Morning News*.)

Southland Center & Sheraton Dallas Hotel, Dallas, Texas

—Dallas News Staff Photo by John Young.

EARLY FLAG RAISING

Southland Center officials marked the erection of the steel for the highest points of the 28-story Sheraton Hotel last week with this novel flag-raising ceremony. With the Texas flag already in place, a crane hoisted the Sheraton flag to the top. The center is to be finished early in 1959.

Sheraton officials were determined not be excluded from the Dallas hotel "boom" and announced plans for its hotel tower just four days after the Statler Hilton's plans were made public in 1950. Designed by Welton Beckett, with Mark Lemmon serving as consulting architect, the Sheraton boasted "Texas-sized" rooms that were larger than the average hotel room and color television sets recessed into the walls. Each floor was decorated in a distinctive color scheme. (Sheraton Corporation.)

The Sheraton opened in April 1959 with a gala much like the Statler Hilton's. Guests arrived from all parts of the country, including Xavier Cugat, Randolph Scott, Howard Keel, Jayne Mansfield, James Garner, Dorothy Malone, and Johnny Weismuller as well as local dignitaries Trammell Crow, Edwin Cox, Fred Florence, Karl Hoblitzelle, and Ben Carpenter. The opening event was sponsored by the Junior League of Dallas and benefited the Southwest Medical Foundation. (*The Dallas Morning News.*)

The Orbit Room cocktail lounge's decor was the space age design of New York artist and decorator Estelle Laverne. Bright blue-green walls were highlighted by a "people in space" motif executed in greens, pinks, and oranges. Carpeting was grass-green, and the upholstery of the bar stools was pink and orange. The chairs were designed by Laverne as well, and four versions were used: lotus, tulip, buttercup, and lily. (*The Dallas Morning News.*)

The Cabana Motor Hotel opened at 899 Stemmons Freeway in 1963 as a "luxury motel" with features "inspired by the lavishness of Roman emperors." The curving facade had a Las Vegas feel, and a huge fountain at the entrance surrounded marble copies of *Venus de Milo* and Michelangelo's *David*. The aqua, white, and gold lobby held a sunken "conversation well" and was carpeted in purple, aqua, and turquoise. The Cabana contained a cocktail lounge, a gourmet restaurant—the Bon Vivant—and a "spectacular" coffee shop—the Hava Java. Adding to this luxury was an Olympic-sized swimming pool that was raised above street level to provide privacy for hotel guests. (Both, Dallas Heritage Village.)

Cabana Motor Hotel, Dallas, Texas

The Cabana hosted the Beatles in September 1964. Although extra security was hired and furniture was removed from public spaces, Dallas teenagers (mostly girls) broke a lobby window and swarmed the hotel. Others stowed away in freight elevators and even crawled through air-conditioning vents in attempts to see the Fab Four, seen here at their Dallas press conference. Officials called the group's one-night stay "Operation Beatle." (Dallas Public Library.)

Actress Doris Day was a principal owner of the Cabana, before it was acquired by Best Western and renamed the DuPont Plaza. Later it was acquired by the Hyatt House hotel chain after foreclosure proceedings in 1969. Dallas County purchased the property, and it was converted into the Bill Decker Detention Center in 1987. (*The Dallas Morning News.*)

Hilton Hotels expanded its Dallas ties when it opened the Dallas Hilton Inn on a 3.5-acre tract at Central Expressway and Mockingbird Lane. Dallas architect Ralph Kelman designed the six-story hotel that included a Trader Vic's Polynesian restaurant. Owing to its proximity to SMU (Southern Methodist University), the building was "topped out" in 1966 with a large branch from a tree that had grown on the university's campus since its founding in 1915. The branch was hauled to the construction site by Peruna, the school's pony mascot. The hotel changed hands in the 1990s, was renamed the Hilltop, and operated until 2005, when it was acquired by Kimpton Hotels, which completely refurbished the hotel and reopened it as the chic Hotel Palomar. (Both, *The Dallas Morning News*.)

The Fairmont was originally envisioned as a hotel-apartment building by developer Edward H. Cary Jr. Construction on the $10-million project, called Cary Plaza, began in February 1961 with plans calling for a 22-story luxury hotel at the corner of Akard Street and Ross Avenue, with an adjoining 18-story apartment building to the north. Architects Harrell and Hamilton's postmodern towers were hailed by local critics for utilizing white Italian Carrara marble on the towers' facades. Despite Cary's ambitious plans, financing troubles halted construction in November 1962, and the half-finished complex sat idle for nearly three years, earning the unflattering nicknames "the twin tombstones" and "the oldest new building in town." In September 1966, plans to transform the stalled project into "the most luxurious hotel in Dallas," as *The Dallas Morning News* described it, were announced by Fairmont Hotel Corporation chairman Richard Swig. (Dallas Public Library.)

The Fairmont's Venetian Room nightclub combined luxury with entertainment by A-list performers, and it was recognized across the county as one of the premier venues between the two coasts. Lou Rawls, Patti Page, Carol Channing, Bobby Short, Peggy Lee, Tina Turner, Johnny Mathis, and Tony Bennett, among others, were regulars. When Peggy Lee arrived for a gig in 1971, she was outraged that the nameplate on her suite stacked the words "Miss Peggy Lee" on three lines. She waited in another suite until the nameplate was changed with the words on one line. The hotel promoted a subscription plan in order to attract a local audience. Attendance was estimated to be "70 percent local community," according to the hotel's management, and "a house guest will have a hard time getting in here." (Left, *The Dallas Morning News*; below, Dallas Public Library.)

AN EXCITING NEW WORLD
OF ENTERTAINMENT PLEASURE
IS BEING CREATED FOR YOU.

WE EXTEND OUR
PERSONAL INVITATION
TO YOU TO BECOME
A MEMBER OF THE

VENETIAN ROOM

AT THE FAIRMONT HOTEL
DALLAS, TEXAS

The Jefferson Dallas Hotel was closed in 1972 by city officials, who purchased it two years later. After it was emptied, plans were drawn up to demolish the building and extend Young Street behind Union Station in a half circle that crossed back over Houston Street and paralleled Wood Street in anticipation of the construction of the huge Reunion Complex, site of the future Hyatt Regency. (*The Dallas Morning News.*)

Initial plans called for the Hotel Dallas to be imploded, but it could not be accomplished without damaging several small buildings on Houston Street, so the building was pulled down in May 1975. As the walls of the old Jefferson came down, the painted "Hotel Scott" sign on its neighbor (now the Hotel Lawrence) was revealed. Today the site contains the Houston Street buildings and a parking lot. (*The Dallas Morning News.*)

By the end of the 1970s, the Baker Hotel, despite the place it held in the hearts of many Dallasites, had become expensive to operate and somewhat run-down. It was purchased by Southwestern Bell in order to construct the 37-story One SBC Plaza (now One AT&T Plaza). In September 1979, a sale of interior furnishings and fixtures was held, and the Baker was razed by implosion in June 1980. (*The Dallas Morning News.*)

It took just a matter of seconds to bring the 55-year-old Baker down. When the dust settled, all that remained was a pile of rubble. For the first time since 1893 when the Oriental Hotel opened "far out in the country," the site would not house a hotel. This photograph shows the Baker's remains in the shadow of its longtime neighbor and sometimes rival, the Adolphus. (*The Dallas Morning News.*)

In 1978, the Hyatt Regency Reunion Dallas became the first major hotel to open in Dallas in 20 years. Its high-profile location, near the Trinity River, the Dallas Convention Center, and the intersection of Interstates I-30 and I-35, made it a dramatic addition to the skyline, and the adjacent Reunion Tower, with its rotating Antares Restaurant at the top, provided Dallas with a bold, new landmark. Welton Beckett Associates designed the hotel and tower, and it was the first of many large building projects downtown that transformed the Dallas skyline in the 1980s. The hotel completed a $70-million expansion in 2001 that added a 30,000-square-foot ballroom and a 40,000-square-foot exhibit hall. (Both, author's collection.)

Hyatt Regency Dallas at Reunion

Sheppard King came to Dallas in the 1880s and made his fortune in the cotton business. In 1908, he built a home north of downtown Dallas near Turtle Creek that was destroyed by fire in 1923. He and his wife, Bertha, traveled through Europe with architect J. Allen Boyle, gathering design ideas for a new home and acquiring architectural elements, including Spanish cathedral doors, ornate columns, and Italian marble. In 1925, their new home was completed. Fashioned in the Italian-Renaissance style, the mansion's features included a fireplace modeled after one in England's Bromley Castle, an oak-paneled library with stained-glass windows, and an unusual, cantilevered staircase. (Both, Rosewood Mansion on Turtle Creek.)

In 1935, the Kings lost their fortune during the Depression, and the home was eventually acquired by oilman Toddie Lee Wynne, who used the home as the headquarters for his American Liberty Oil Company. In 1979, Caroline Rose Hunt founded the Rosewood Property Company and purchased the mansion, expanding it in a $21-million project and transforming the home into the Mansion on Turtle Creek. The home's veranda, library, and living room became part of the hotel's dining room, and the fur and silver vault was reconfigured as a wine cellar. The Mansion opened in 1981 to critical acclaim, and it was awarded the Keystone Award by the Historic Preservation League of Dallas. In 1989, the Mansion was awarded a five-star rating by Mobil Travel Guide, and in 1991, the American Automobile Association honored the hotel with five diamonds, its highest rating, making it Texas's only five-star, five-diamond hotel. (Rosewood Mansion on Turtle Creek.)

Dallas added another large hotel complex in 1979 when the Anatole Hotel opened along Stemmons Freeway. The addition of the Hyatt Reunion and the Anatole made it possible for Dallas to host its first national political convention in 1984, when Republicans convened to nominate Pres. Ronald Reagan for a second term. The Anatole was headquarters for the Reagans, and one of the most memorable moments of the convention came when Nancy Reagan, addressing the delegates at Reunion Arena, turned to a gigantic television screen and waved to President Reagan, who watched the proceedings with Vice President Bush in the Anatole's Presidential Suite. (Both, *The Dallas Morning News*.)

The Anatole was acquired by Hilton Hotels and continues to be a favored site for large conventions and local civic events. Its proximity to the Dallas Trade Mart and Market Center, along with its 344,000 square feet of meeting and exhibition space, makes it a popular choice for trade shows and markets. (Hilton Hotels Corporation.)

In 1995, the Southland Center, including the Sheraton Hotel, closed as an office complex, reopening as the Harvey House Hotel. In 2000, Adam's Mark Hotels purchased the Harvey House and completed a $30-million overhaul, converting the entire complex into hotel space, making it the largest in Dallas. Sheraton Hotels returned to the site in 2008, acquiring the Adam's Mark and returning the Sheraton name to the Dallas skyline. (Author's photograph.)

Rosewood Hotels and Resorts opened its fourth luxury hotel, the Rosewood Crescent Hotel, in late December 1986. The company's philosophy, guided by founder Caroline Rose Hunt, was to create luxurious, residential-style hotels that offered high attention to detail and exceptional personalized service. The Crescent Court complex includes the hotel, a large mansard-roofed office complex, and retail space housing high-end shops and restaurants. Crescent Court was designed by John Burgee Architects with Phillip Johnson and became the genesis for redevelopment of Dallas's Uptown area. The Crescent Court was the last large hotel opened in Dallas before the economy crumbled when the price of oil plummeted in the mid-1980s. (Rosewood Crescent Hotel.)

Six

RISE AND SHINE

Five years from now, you're not even going to recognize downtown.
—Rob Gormley, general manager of W Dallas Victory, May 2006

The question remains: If we build it, will they come?
—State Representative Steve Wolens, 2003

Recent years have seen the openings of the W Hotel at Victory Park and the Ritz-Carlton in Uptown. Historic structures have been repurposed and given new life: the Magnolia (the former Magnolia Oil Building) and Hotel Joule (formerly the Dallas National Bank Building) have become places that acknowledge the past but exude a chic, young energy. The Adam's Mark Hotel was purchased by Sheraton and underwent an extensive renovation. Hotel Belmont in Oak Cliff and Hotel Palomar on the edge of the Park Cities had declined over the years but were painstakingly restored and attract savvy travelers and local hipsters. One-hundred years ago, hotel patrons were attracted by fireproof buildings and elevators, where today wi-fi connections and infinity pools are the new marketing hooks.

The new hotels, particularly those downtown, were made possible through efforts by preservationists and local government, who have attracted development with tax incentives and have spurred revitalization of the area, a longtime goal of city officials. Efforts have been largely successful, but there have been setbacks as well: following the terrorist attacks of 9/11, occupancy rates plummeted but slowly recovered, and the recent economic downturn led to the scrapping of plans to develop a Mandarin Oriental Hotel.

What lies ahead for Dallas hotels? Ground has been broken on the convention center hotel, Dallas will host its first Super Bowl in 2011, which will shine national attention on its facilities, and there is talk of hosting another major political convention in 2012. The history of Dallas hotels continues to be written.

The Hotel St. Germain (above) was built as a private home by John Patrick Murphy in 1906 and was occupied by members of the Murphy family until the 1960s. After it was sold, it housed, among other things, a bar and a computer school until it was purchased by Claire Heymann in 1989. Heymann restored the building and opened it as the St. Germain Hotel, an intimate upscale hotel in 1991. The Westin City Center (below) opened as the Intercontinental Hotel and was later purchased by Omni Hotels and then Westin Hotels. Its unique space, surrounding and indoor ice skating rink, and shops and restaurants have made it a popular hotel for people visiting the city for business as well as for downtown workers who lunch and shop here. (Above, *The Dallas Morning News*; below, Westin City Center Dallas.)

Revitalization of the area northwest of downtown was spawned by the opening of the American Airlines Center in 2001. Starwood Hotels and Resorts began construction of W Dallas Victory in 2005, and it opened in 2006. The property contains hotel rooms up to the 15th floor and transitions to residences between the 16th and 33rd floors that offer sweeping views of the city. (Both, W Dallas Victory.)

The Joule is located in the former Dallas National Bank building, which was constructed in 1927. Coburn, Smith, and Evans were the architects of the 16-story Gothic steel-framed building that was faced with granite, Bedford stone, and terra-cotta. In 2007, the building underwent an extensive and sensitive restoration, and the building became the home to the Joule, a sophisticated, contemporary hotel. The Joule is an excellent example of the merits of preserving our historic structures. (Both, the Joule.)

The Magnolia Hotel has also brought an iconic Dallas building back to life. Located in the landmark Pegasus-crowned Magnolia Building, the Magnolia offers 330 upscale rooms in the heart of downtown. When the building, designed by Sir Alfred Bossom, opened in 1922, it was the tallest west of the Mississippi. The 24th floor is dubbed the Historic Floor and features doors with the original glass transoms, marble wainscoting, and wood paneling and floors. (Dallas Magnolia Hotel.)

Ritz-Carlton made its debut in 2007, opening in the vibrant Uptown area, and its presence illustrates Dallas's status as a major international city. The only Ritz-Carlton in Texas, the hotel contains 218 rooms, a popular spa, and Fearing's, a gourmet restaurant overseen by renowned chef Dean Fearing. An adjacent Ritz-Carlton Residences tower is expected to be completed in 2009. (Author's photograph.)

Dallas's hotels are among the most cutting edge in the nation and are very much in touch with trends in food, culture, and tastes. The Fairmont Dallas is the first hotel in the city to grow many of the herbs and vegetables used in the hotel's kitchens. The Fairmont's chef, j. w. Foster, is committed to the hotel's commitment to utilizing local, organic, and sustainable products. (*The Dallas Morning News.*)

Mayor Tom Leppert celebrated the defeat of Proposition 1 in May 2009 that would have prevented municipal ownership of a hotel. Leppert campaigned vigorously for the measure's defeat and had the backing of most of the city council. A strong and well-funded opposition movement, Citizens Against the Taxpayer Owned Hotel, appeared to lead in the debate but in the end narrowly lost, and the defeat paved the way for construction of a convention center hotel. (*The Dallas Morning News.*)

BIBLIOGRAPHY

Carmack, Liz. *Historic Hotels of Texas*. College Station: Texas A&M University Press, 2007.

Childers, Sam. "Historic Hotels of Dallas 1890–1956." *Legacies: A History Journal for Dallas and North Central Texas*, spring 2007: 58–61.

———. "The Place to Be: Dallas's Fairmont Hotel and Venetian Room." *Legacies: A History Journal for Dallas and North Central Texas*, spring 2009: 36–49.

Enstam, Elizabeth York. "Boardinghouses in Dallas: Frontier Institutions." *Heritage News*, fall 1984: 9–11.

Fuller, Larry ed. *The American Institute of Architects Guide to Dallas Architecture*. New York: McGraw Hill Construction Information Group, 1999.

Hazel, Michael V. "Early Hotels in Dallas: Striving to Meet the Needs of Travelers." *Heritage News*, winter 1983–1984: 4–5.

———. *Dallas*. Austin, TX: Texas State Historical Association, 1997.

———. *Historic Photos of Dallas*. Nashville, TN: Turner Publishing Company, 2006.

Jones, Dwayne. "From Camps to Courts: Dallas Tourist Accommodations in the Early Twentieth Century." *Legacies: A History Journal for Dallas and North Central Texas*, spring 1995: 24–31.

McDonald, William. *Dallas Rediscovered*. Dallas, TX: Dallas Historical Society, 1978.

Payne, Darwin. *Big D: Triumphs and Troubles of an American Supercity in the 20th Century*. Dallas, TX: Three Forks Press, 1994.

———. *Dallas: An Illustrated History*. Woodland Hills: Windsor Publications, Inc., 1982.

Preservation Dallas and Dallas Heritage Village. *Dallas Landmarks*. Charleston, SC: Arcadia Publishing, 2008.

Ragsdale, Kenneth. *Centennial '36: The Year America Discovered Texas*. College Station, TX: Texas A&M University Press, 1987.

Rice, Mark. *Downtown Dallas: Romantic Past, Modern Renaissance*. Dallas, TX: Brown Books Publishing Group, 2007.

Rogers, John W. *The Lusty Texans of Dallas*. New York: E. P. Dunton and Company Inc., 1951.

Rugh, Susan. *Are We There Yet? The Golden Age of American Family Vacations*. Lawrence, KS: University Press of Kansas, 2008.

Sandoval-Strausz, A. K. *Hotel: An American History*. New York: A. K. Sandoval-Strausz, 2007.

The Dallas Morning News Archive, http://infoweb.newsbank.com

www.arcadiapublishing.com

MAP SEARCH

Discover books about the town where you grew up, the cities where your friends and families live, the town where your parents met, or even that retirement spot you've been dreaming about. Our Web site provides history lovers with exclusive deals, advanced notification about new titles, e-mail alerts of author events, and much more.

MADE IN THE
 **USA**

Arcadia Publishing, the leading local history publisher in the United States, is committed to making history accessible and meaningful through publishing books that celebrate and preserve the heritage of America's people and places. Consistent with our mission to preserve history on a local level, this book was printed in South Carolina on American-made paper and manufactured entirely in the United States.

This book carries the accredited Forest Stewardship Council (FSC) label and is printed on 100 percent FSC-certified paper. Products carrying the FSC label are independently certified to assure consumers that they come from forests that are managed to meet the social, economic, and ecological needs of present and future generations.

FSC
Mixed Sources
Product group from well-managed forests and other controlled sources

Cert no. SW-COC-001530
www.fsc.org
© 1996 Forest Stewardship Council

Find Your Place in History.